EVALUATING VIEWPOINTS:
CRITICAL THINKING IN
UNITED STATES HISTORY SERIES

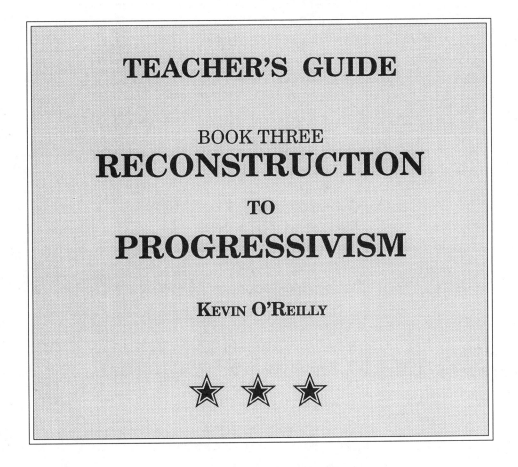

TEACHER'S GUIDE

BOOK THREE
RECONSTRUCTION
TO
PROGRESSIVISM

KEVIN O'REILLY

★ ★ ★

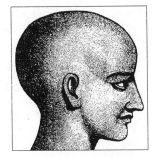

© 1983, 1991
CRITICAL THINKING PRESS & SOFTWARE
(formerly Midwest Publications)
P.O. Box 448 • Pacific Grove • CA 93950-0448
Phone 800-458-4849 • FAX 408-393-3277
ISBN 0-89455-418-2
Printed in the United States of America

TABLE OF CONTENTS

ABOUT THE AUTHOR

Kevin O'Reilly is a social studies teacher at Hamilton-Wenham Regional High School in Massachusetts. He was named by *Time* magazine and the National Council for the Social Studies as the 1986 Outstanding Social Studies Teacher in the United States. In addition to these four volumes on Critical Thinking in Unites States History, Mr. O'Reilly is the coauthor of *Critical Viewing: Stimulant to Critical Thinking* (also published by Midwest Publications/Critical Thinking Press & Software), and the author of "Escalation," a computer simulation on the Vietnam War (Kevin O'Reilly, 6 Mason Street, Beverly, MA 01915). Mr. O'Reilly, who has a Master of Arts Degree in History, is an editor of the *New England Journal of History*. He conducts workshops throughout the United States on critical thinking, critical viewing, and decision-making.

FOR

My sons
Brian and Sean

ACKNOWLEDGMENTS

I would like to thank the following for their help: Gordon Library for helping me track down sources on the Chicago Stockyards (Lesson 17); Beverly Library for helping me research the Fourteenth Amendment (Lesson 6) and John D. Rockefeller (Lesson 15 and 16); the Library of Congress for finding numerous pictures for the book (Lessons 9 and 17); and Historical Pictures Service for cartoons on immigration (Lesson 26).

INTRODUCTION

Overview of This Section

This teacher's guide contains an introduction; reproducible introductory lessons for each skill covered in the series; suggested teaching strategies and answers for each lesson in the student text; and test questions. The introduction includes:

1. an introduction to the process of critical thinking;

2. a rationale for the series;

3. a description of the role of the teacher, including an overview of the *Teacher's Guide*, suggestions for classroom methods for teaching critical thinking in history, and various suggestions for evaluating student progress;

4. a description of the role of the student, including an overview of the student text;

5. a chart of the scope and sequences of skills developed in this text;

6. a bibliography of sources on critical·thinking.

What Is Critical Thinking?

One author calls critical thinking "reasoned judgment." For the purposes of this series, critical thinking is *judging* the worth of claims or arguments. It involves judgment, assessment, and evaluation. The critical thinker has a healthy skepticism and asks probing questions; the non-critical thinker is likely to jump to conclusions and believe whatever is claimed.

Critical thinking is not the same as creative thinking, brainstorming, problem solving, decision making, conceptualizing, or Bloom's taxonomy—although it is involved in the judgment phase of problem solving and decision making. Neither is it the same as asking students to compare and contrast or to categorize—for those activities do not require students to evaluate the comparisons made or categories delineated.

Only level six (evaluation) of Bloom's taxonomy involves critical thinking. Level four (analysis) is so important to evaluation of arguments, however, that some of these skills are also directly taught in these books.

The following analysis and evaluation skills are included in the series.

> ### — Analysis Skills —
>
> - Differentiating between conclusions and reasons
> - Identifying types of reasoning
> - Identifying sources of information
> - Classifying parts of an argument based on cue words, value words, emotional words, and change-of-direction words
> - Identifying assumptions and value judgments
>
> ### — Evaluation Skills —
>
> - Evaluating the relevance of reasons to conclusions
> - Evaluating types of reasoning
> - Evaluating sources
> - Evaluating assumptions and value judgments

Overall, then, the critical thinker asks, "Why should I believe this?" and offers reasoned judgments in answer to that question. These books are meant to arm students with the critical-thinking skills necessary to make reasoned judgments, to prod them into asking questions, and to give them the confidence both to ask questions and to offer judgments.

About This Series

This four-volume series, Evaluating Viewpoints: Critical Thinking in United States History, is intended to improve critical thinking through evaluation of conflicting viewpoints of United States history. The books are chronological, each covering a particular time period.

Book 1: Colonies Through Constitution (1492–1789)

Book 2: New Republic Through Civil War (1790–1865)

Book 3: Reconstruction Through Progressivism (1865–1914)

Book 4: Spanish-American War Through Vietnam War (1900–1980)

There is not, however, chronological coverage within each book. Each lesson is a self-contained problem that can be "plugged in" at any point in a corresponding history unit.

These books are thus meant to supplement other curriculum materials, not to be the sole text for a course.

As mentioned in the introduction of the student text, the root word of history is *story*. In this series, emphasis is on helping students see that the "story" of history can be told in different ways and that values, attitudes, perceptions, and selection all shape the way people see the past. These books are intended to show students that historical subject matter is not some unchanging, agreed upon, and complete subject to be memorized, but rather is changing, selective, fragmentary, and open to interpretation.

The target of this series is understanding, not memorizing. Studies in cognitive psychology indicate that memorization lasts only a short time. Focusing on problems, thinking, and understanding helps students remember the content of history much longer.

The Role of the Teacher
About the Teacher's Guide

The *Teacher's Guide* contains:
1. an introduction to the series;
2. reproducible worksheets for introducing each skill;
3. objectives, teaching ideas, and suggested answers for each lesson;
4. possible test questions and suggested answers.

Twelve skill worksheets are included in the *Teacher's Guide* of each book in the series. These can be used to promote a questioning attitude (Worksheet A), introduce particular skills (Worksheets B–J), or serve as general worksheets for evaluating any film or written argument (Worksheets K–L). The teaching ideas and the suggested answers are intended as guidance for the teacher, not as rigid lesson plans or right answers. The emphasis is on thinking, not on "correct" answers.

A key element in the emphasis on teaching, practicing, and repeating critical thinking skills is the "Scope and Sequence of Skills" chart on pages 12–13. Once you have decided which skills to teach, this chart will serve as a quick reference to their location in each book and to help you select appropriate lessons for practice and repetition. Values are included under "Assumptions" in the scope-and-sequence chart, since they are a kind of assumption about the way the world should be. Those lessons focusing on values are marked with a "v."

Some skills are not represented on the scope-and-sequence chart. Although these skills are not **explicitly** taught in any lesson in the book, they are a part of many of the problem lessons. For example, finding the main idea is an important part of evaluating the interpretations in the book. The importance of using key words for encoding parts of arguments is also a part of many problem lessons, but is never explicitly taught in any specific lesson. For further information on critical thinking, refer to the Bibliography of Sources on Critical Thinking on page 11 in this book.

Classroom Methods for Teaching Critical Thinking in History

Unlike other anthologies of opposing viewpoints, this series focuses on how to analyze and evaluate arguments. In improving athletic performance, coaches know that a systematic approach works best. Skills must be broken down and their components explained; the athlete has to try the skill with the guidance of the coach; the athlete must repeatedly practice the skill; and, finally, the skills must be applied in the athletic contest. This same method is used in these books to teach skills of critical thinking. Each skill is broken down and explained in the "Guide to Critical Thinking"; with the guidance of the teacher and/or other students, the student tries the skill on worksheets; additional worksheets provide practice as the student repeats the skill; and, finally, the student applies the skill to new opposing-viewpoint problems. This pattern of skill instruction is outlined below.

Pattern of Skill Instruction

1. INITIAL PROBLEM

In the books in this series, students are confronted with a historical problem from the student text. Since the problem consists of opposing viewpoints, students are forced to evaluate the viewpoints to arrive at a conclusion. This raises the need to learn to think critically in deciding which viewpoint to believe.

2. FAMILIAR EXAMPLE

The teacher gives the class an everyday problem, either from the "Guide to Critical Thinking" or an introductory worksheet, on the skill involved in step 1. Familiar examples make it easier for students to learn the skill.

3. METACOGNITION

This step offers direct teaching of analysis and/or evaluation skills. As the class discusses answers to the familiar problem in step 2, they discuss how class members arrived at their answers. The focus here is on *metacognition*—thinking about thinking, not about the content of the problem—and the components are taught directly. What is involved in performing the skill? What are the steps in the skill? What are the criteria for evaluation? A diagram of the steps or criteria is then posted in the classroom and/or drawn in the "skills" section of students' notebooks. Ideally, the students, guided by the teacher, will identify the components of the skill; those the class cannot identify can be taught directly by the teacher using the "Guide to Critical Thinking."

4. GUIDED PRACTICE

The students are referred back to the historical problem in step 1 and directed to discuss its evaluation in light of the skill they have learned. The students employ the skill on the problem and on worksheets with the guidance of the teacher and other students.

5. MASTERY

Students repeatedly practice the skill on additional worksheets and in class discussions.

6. EXTENSION

As the course progresses, students extend the skill as they apply it to new historical problems.

Class Discussions

From this emphasis on specific critical thinking skills, it can be seen that class discussions of the opposing viewpoints presented in the books are not to be free-for-alls, where all opinions are equally good. Students are expected to employ the skills learned in previous classes, to question assertions made by their classmates, and to defend their own assertions with evidence and reasons. This is a far cry from an emphasis on right answers. In this series, the emphasis is on good thinking, not on right answers.

Adaptation

Obviously, some of the lessons in this text are more difficult than others. Teachers can make easy lessons more challenging by eliminating step-by-step questions or worksheets or by making students produce their own examples to illustrate particular skills. Lessons that are too difficult for some classes can be made easier by doing only a portion of the lesson, by focusing on only a single skill, or by giving students the step-by-step worksheet on the topic. Refer to teaching suggestions on specific lessons for further guidance in the difficulty level of each lesson within this book.

Using the "Guide to Critical Thinking"

The "Guide to Critical Thinking," the first unit in each student text, is meant to help teachers with the direct instruction of key elements of the various critical thinking skills. These key skills are summarized in the chart on pages 12–13.

Although the Guide touches on numerous skills related to the evaluation of interpretations or arguments, it focuses on four of these skills: evaluation of evidence, evaluation of cause-and-effect reasoning, evaluation of comparison reasoning (analogy), and evaluation of generalizations. A grasp of these four argument components is an enormous help in the students' ability to think critically.

The section on *evidence* emphasizes the idea of sources of information. Rather than distinguishing between evidence, which has a source, and information, which provides no source, students are simply instructed to ask, "Is there a source?" whenever they encounter information in support of a claim. If not, they are to note that weakness. If yes, they are to evaluate it. Introductory Worksheet B (pp. 33–34 in this book) provides a concrete problem for determining and evaluating evidence.

In the section on *reasoning*, it is again important to note that students are not only taught to identify the type of reasoning but also to evaluate it. It is not enough that a student says, "This is a cause-and-effect argument." The student must also say whether it is a strong or weak cause-and-effect argument and give reasons for saying so. A concrete problem for introducing cause-and-effect reasoning can be found in the teaching ideas for Introductory Worksheet E (pp. 39–40 in this book).

The section on *evaluating comparisons* (analogies) is not the same as the activity of compare and contrast. This critical thinking skill focuses on evaluating comparison arguments, or what is sometimes called analogic reasoning. For example, asking students to compare and contrast the fighting in Nicaragua in the 1980s with the Vietnam War is very different from asking them to evaluate the argument "The United States should not be involved in fighting in Nicaragua because it will turn into another Vietnam." Although both assignments involve basic knowledge of the two situations, the second assignment requires students to identify the type of reasoning used and to implement comparison and contrast without being cued to do so (as in the first assignment). A concrete problem for introducing comparison reasoning is in the teaching ideas for Introductory Worksheet F (pp. 41–42 in this book).

The term *generalization*, rather than *sample reasoning*, is used for this skill. Use the pizza example on page 8 of the student book as a concrete problem for introducing generalizations. Ask "Suppose you bit into a pizza and the bite was cold. What might you conclude about the pizza?" The strength of a generalization can be determined by asking, "How large and representative is the sample?" Some people, however, believe that randomness is better than representativeness as a method for achieving an accurate sample. In any event, you might want to mention to your students that randomness is also a commonly accepted method of sampling.

Fallacies, although included with each type of reasoning, are not emphasized either in the Guide or in the lessons. Simply teaching students a few questions to ask (and the willingness to ask them) within several broad areas of reasoning will usually be more helpful than teaching them a larger number of fallacies and having them try to fit real arguments into one of these fallacies.

Several points emphasized in the ARMEAR model on page 18 in the student text are not emphasized elsewhere in the Guide. One such point is questions about the author (A); the second is relevant information (R). Students should be taught to bring any information that might be relevant to bear on the topic. They may, of course, have difficulty determining what is relevant. Additionally, they are not in the habit of seeing the relevance of one topic to another. To encourage the habit of thinking about what might be relevant to a historical problem, a number of lessons include relevant information sheets. Students who don't use the sheets can't do a complete analysis of the arguments. Encouraging this habit of calling on what they know helps students view history as a fund of knowledge to be drawn upon to help provide perspective on other, similar issues. History thereby becomes more meaningful.

Skill Transfer

Many of the worksheets contain both everyday and historic argument examples. This mixture is intended to promote transfer of the skills learned into other areas of the students' lives. Teachers can facilitate this transfer of critical thinking skills learned in history class to other subject areas by having students debate topics then analyze the reasoning they used in the debate. When students realize that they use the same reasoning elements in their own thinking, they are more likely to transfer them into other areas of their lives. Another important method for promoting skill transfer is to listen carefully to student chatter before class starts. If you can ask a question on the use of a particular type of reasoning on a topic heard in a student conversation, you will connect the skill learned in history to the students' everyday lives.

Evaluation

Test questions are provided at the end of this teacher's guide, and the many problem sheets in the student text provide even more possible test questions. Of course, teachers should consider the viewpoints in the longer problems for essay assignments. These can be evaluation essays, such as "Evaluate Historian A's argument on immigration. In your essay identify and evaluate two pieces of evidence and two types of reasoning."

WRITING AND THINKING

Writing skills are an important part of this curriculum, and students should be held accountable for their critical thinking skills when they write any essay assignment. A sample student assignment might be, "Write a minimum 250-word essay on the main cause of the American Revolution. In your essay you are to show what makes a strong cause, support your case with one piece of evidence, and explain why this is strong evidence." Students must learn how to construct strong arguments in addition to evaluating the arguments made by others.

Overview of Book 3

Book 3 is comprised of the "Guide to Critical Thinking" (Unit 1), ten introductory lessons, and twenty-seven lessons divided into three units. Lessons 1–9 are in the Reconstruction Unit; Lessons 10–18 in the Industrialization and Response Unit; Lessons 19–27 in the Workers, Immigrants, and Farmers in the 1800s Unit. The table of contents and the scope-and-sequence chart show the specific topic and the emphasized skills of each lesson.

> Lessons with titles phrased as questions are historical problems, rather than worksheets. These problems involve numerous skills and focus on historical issues; worksheets focus on a specific skill and mix everyday, modern examples with historical content.

The first four skills in the scope-and-sequence chart (evidence, cause and effect, comparison, and generalization) involve both identification and evaluation. A few lessons focus on just identification or evaluation, but most consider both. Values are included under assumptions in the scope-and-sequence chart since values are assumptions about the way the world should be.

Some skills are not represented in the scope-and-sequence chart as they are not explicitly taught in any of the lessons. They are a part of the historical-problem lessons, however. Finding the main idea and using key words for encoding parts of arguments are two such skills.

Some teachers will prefer to use just the historical-problem lessons (Lessons 6–9, 14–18, and 23–27). These problem lessons can be used to teach a variety of skills and are interesting topics to study. Worksheet lessons, on the other hand, provide practice in particular skills which help students do more complete analyses of the interpretations in the problem lessons. The worksheet lessons provide sequencing of each skill.

The list of major sources used (pp. 195–97 in the student text) shows that the viewpoints in Book 3 are based on the views of major historians: Kenneth Stampp, William Dunning, and Eric Foner on Reconstruction; Adam Smith, Willian Graham Sumner, Richard T. Ely, and Thorstein Veblen on laissez-faire; Ida Tarbell and Allan Nevins on John D. Rockefeller; Richard Hofstadter on the Progressive Movement; and Milton Meltzer on the Pullman Strike.

While these are all well known interpretations, some are highly controversial. People may argue that some of the interpretations are quite fanciful, not credible enough to bring to student attention. But if the interpretations are weak, let the students recognize their weaknesses. Good arguments are judged good because they are stronger than bad arguments. Students need to encounter and evaluate both. Because of this, there are no standard right and wrong answers to the problems in this book.

The Role of the Student

The student book contains the "Guide to Critical Thinking" and twenty-seven lessons involving critical thinking. The "Guide to Critical Thinking" is intended to be used when students have a need to learn the components of a particular skill. While some may find it worthwhile to read through the whole Guide to get an overview of the skills involved in argument evaluation, it is not recommended that students study all the various skills at once. Rather, they should refer to the part of the Guide that explains the skill they are currently learning.

The historical lessons consist of both a short problem section for practicing skills (1–2 pages each) and longer historical problems (2–32 pages each) with opposing viewpoints. Paragraphs in longer viewpoints are numbered to make discussion and referencing easier.

Particular skills, especially generalizations and cause-and-effect reasoning, are explained with visual models. These have proven helpful for many students, some of whom regularly use them to help evaluate arguments on tests.

These books focus on formulating good arguments as well as evaluating arguments offered by others. In this way, students should begin to question their own assumptions, points of view, and prejudices. This self-criticism, referred to by Richard Paul as "critical thinking in the strong sense," is an important, if difficult, goal to achieve.

Students should begin to see historical knowledge as changing, selective, fragmentary, and open to question. This change in student attitudes about the nature of historical knowledge (epistemology) is as important as their mastery of critical thinking skills. Beginning with Worksheet A, students should be encouraged, even expected, to question viewpoints presented. The problem format helps students see history the way it really is and to ask questions. It also makes history much more interesting.

Bibliography of Sources on Critical Thinking

Beyer, Barry. *Practical Strategies for the Teaching of Thinking.* Boston: Allyn and Bacon, 1987.

———— "Teaching Critical Thinking: A Direct Approach." *Social Education* 49 (April 1985): 297–303.

Bloch, Marc. *The Historian's Craft.* New York: Random House, 1953.

Bloom, Benjamin S., ed. *Taxonomy of Educational Objectives, Handbook I: Cognitive Domain.* New York: David McKay, 1956.

Carr, Edward Harlett. *What Is History?* New York: Random House, 1961.

Copi, Irving. *Introduction to Logic.* 5th ed. New York: Macmillan, 1978.

Costa, Arthur. "Teaching For, Of, and About Thinking." In *Developing Minds: A Resource Book for Teaching Thinking.* Edited by Arthur L. Costa, 20–24. Alexandria, VA: Association for Supervision and Curriculum Development, 1985.

———— and Lawrence Lowery. *Techniques for Teaching Thinking.* Pacific Grove, CA: Midwest, 1989.

Crossley, David J., and Peter Wilson. *How to Argue.* New York: Random House, 1979.

Fisher, David Hackett. *Historians' Fallacies: Toward a Logic of Historical Thought.* New York: Harper and Row, 1970.

Gustavson, Carl. *A Preface to History.* New York: McGraw-Hill, 1955.

Norris, Stephen. "The Reliability of Observation Statements." *Rational Thinking Reports,* No. 4. Urbana, IL: University of Illinois, 1979.

———— and Robert Ennis. *Evaluating Critical Thinking.* Pacific Grove, CA: Midwest, 1989.

O'Reilly, Kevin. "Teaching Critical Thinking in High School U.S. History." *Social Education* 49 (April 1985): 281–4.

———— "Vietnam: A Case Study for Critical Thinking" (videotape). Pleasantville, NY: Educational Audiovisual, 1989.

Paul, Richard. "Critical Thinking: Fundamental to Education for a Free Society." *Educational Leadership* 42 (September 1984): 4–14.

Roden, Philip. *The Elusive Truth.* Glenview, IL: Scott-Foresman, 1973.

Sanders, Norris. *Classroom Questions: What Kinds?* New York: Harper and Row, 1966.

Swartz, Robert and D. N. Perkins. *Teaching Thinking: Issues and Approaches.* Pacific Grove, CA: Midwest, 1989.

Weddle, Perry. *Argument: A Guide to Critical Thinking.* New York: McGraw-Hill, 1977.

Scope and Sequence of Skills • Book 3

Abbreviations used in this chart are as follows: (**TG**)–Teacher's Guide; (**GTC**)–"Guide to Critical Thinking," Unit 1 in Student Book; (**d**)–Debating reasoning; (**v**)–Values; (**f**)–Frame of reference.

Lesson	Topic	Evidence	Cause/Effect	Comparison	Generalization	Assumption	Relevant Information	Proof and Debating
Concrete Example		TG 14	TG 19	TG 39	GCT 8	—	—	—
Explanation		GCT 2	GCT 5	GCT 7	GCT 8	GCT 15	GCT 18	GCT 11

Introductory Worksheets

Lesson	Topic	Evidence	Cause/Effect	Comparison	Generalization	Assumption	Relevant Information	Proof and Debating
A	Bermuda Triangle	■	■		■			
B, C, D	Evaluating Evidence	■				■		
E	Cause and Effect Reasoning		■					
F, G	Evaluating Comparisons			■				
H	Evaluating Generalizations				■			
I, J	Identifying Assumptions					■		

Reconstruction

Lesson	Topic	Evidence	Cause/Effect	Comparison	Generalization	Assumption	Relevant Information	Proof and Debating
1	Reconstruction	■						
2	Reconstruction	■						
3	Reconstruction	■						
4	Reconstruction		■					
5	Reconstruction	■			■			
6	Fourteenth Amendment						■	
7	Reconstruction Legislation	■	■		■	■		
8	Reconstruction Governments	■	■	■	■	■		(d)
9	Political Cartoons	■						

Scope and Sequence of Skills • Book 3 (continued)

Industrializtion and Response

Lesson	Topic	Evidence	Cause/Effect	Comparison	Generalization	Assumption	Relevant Information	Proof and Debating
10	Industrialists	▓						
11	Gilded Age			▓				
12	Industrialization		▓					
13	Gilded Age	▓	▓	▓	▓			
14	Social Darwinism	▓				▓	▓	
15	John D. Rockefeller		▓	▓		▓ (f)		
16	John D. Rockefeller	▓	▓	▓	▓	▓ (v)	▓	
17	The Jungle	▓		▓	▓	▓ (f)		
18	Progressive Movement	▓				▓		▓ (d)

Workers, Immigrants, and Farmers in the Late 1800s

Lesson	Topic	Evidence	Cause/Effect	Comparison	Generalization	Assumption	Relevant Information	Proof and Debating
19	Labor		▓					
20	Workers and Immigrants		▓		▓			
21	Workers and Immigrants			▓				
22	Workers and Immigrants				▓			▓
23	Urban Bosses	▓		▓	▓			
24	Pullman Strike	▓	▓	▓	▓	▓		▓ (d)
25	Immigration	▓	▓	▓	▓	▓	▓	▓
26	Immigration	▓					▓	
27	Omaha Platform (Populists)					▓	▓	

©1991 Midwest Publications/Critical Thinking Press & Software, P.O. Box 448, Pacific Grove, CA 93950

UNIT 1
INTRODUCTORY LESSONS FOR SKILL DEVELOPMENT

Worksheet A: The Bermuda Triangle

Objectives

To increase skepticism of what is read, seen, or heard
To develop inclination and ability to question statements

Teaching Ideas
PREPARATION

Give students copies of the first page of the worksheet (page 31) and ask them to write their reaction to it. Do not allow discussion at this point. Check to make sure everyone has written something. If some students say they don't understand what to write, tell them to write down how they feel about the reading, but don't go into any more detail. The whole idea is to avoid letting them know what reactions you are looking for.

USING THE WORKSHEET

Some students will accept the argument in the handout without any criticisms. Many students feel that anything written down must be true. When the discussion begins they will see that some of their classmates were more skeptical and that the argument should not have been blindly accepted.

When you distribute copies of the Relevant Information sheet (page 32), this lesson in skepticism should be reinforced. After students read the relevant information, the author's argument should look very weak.

EXTENDING THE LESSON

This reading might also be used to teach a number of other skills, such as finding the main idea, identifying value and emotional words, identifying assumptions and fallacies, and evaluating evidence.

Suggested Analysis

The author argues that one hundred ships go down each year, but does not compare that to the number of ships in the area (ten thousand distress calls) or to the number of sinkings in other areas of the ocean.

In paragraph 6 the author uses the "leading question technique" when he asks why pilot Cosner did not go on Flight 19. Maybe Cosner was constipated or had the flu. The later suggestion that he had a "peculiar feeling" is not really argued or supported by evidence. Similarly, the author suggests that the Navy is covering up the situation by not saying anything about it. But maybe the Navy has not bothered to deny it because the whole theory is so ridiculous.

Worksheet B: Evaluating Evidence

Objectives

To increase ability in identifying evidence
To increase ability in evaluating evidence

Teaching Ideas

INTRODUCING THE SKILL

To introduce the skills of identifying and evaluating evidence, take five students into the hallway, out of the class's sight, and tell them they are going to role play a murder. Have three students stay near your classroom door, one student go 25 feet down the hall in one direction, and the other student go 25 feet in the opposite direction. Tell them they are to watch carefully. Hand one of the three students by the door a pen and tell him or her to point it at one of the other students in the hall and yell, "Bang!" Tell the "murdered" student to fall down.

Bring the five students back together, and tell them the rest of the class is going to ask them questions to figure out who committed the crime. Only the murderer may lie; the witnesses (everyone else in the hall) must tell the truth. Tell the other witnesses they must tell everything they know. They are not to hide information or try to confuse the class.

When using this in class, substitute the corresponding student name for each of the roles in italics.

Re-enter the classroom with the five students. Tell the class that *the victim* was just killed, and have that person sit down. Tell the class that their task is to figure out who did it by questioning the four witnesses. [At some point a student may ask where the murder weapon is. If so, produce the pen (tell them it's a poison-dart gun) and ask if they have any questions about the weapon. If they ask about fingerprints, say that only *the murderer's* fingerprints are on it.] Later, tell the class that you have a letter, dated a month ago, written by *the murderer* to a close friend saying he or she was going to get even with *the victim*. Don't be discouraged if the students don't ask very good questions. Even advanced classes have had difficulty with this introductory exercise.

After ten to fifteen minutes, tell the class that you're going to stop talking about who committed the murder and, instead, talk about the skill involved in trying to decide who did it. This is the metacognitive stage. Ask the class what they think evidence is. [Based on this activity: statements by witnesses, objects that were part of the event, or written documents.]

The best way to get at the criteria for evaluating evidence is to ask the general question: How did you decide which evidence to believe? This way the class will generate the criteria themselves. If the general question proves too difficult you can ask more specific questions:

Ask the class why they didn't believe *the murderer* when s/he said s/he didn't do it. [S/he had a reason to lie to protect him- or herself.] Suppose *the murderer* said *a witness* did it, and *that witness* said *the murderer* did it, and that's all the class knew. Could they have told who was guilty? [No.] So why did they believe *that witness* over *the murderer*? [Because other witnesses supported *that witness's* version by saying *the murderer* did it.] Suppose a third witness was around the corner when the murder occurred. Would that strengthen or weaken his/her evidence? [Weaken it.] Why? [The testimony is now given by someone who did not see the crime—a secondary source.] Is *the murderer* more likely to tell the truth in the trial or in a letter to a friend? [This is tricky, but the private letter is generally more reliable.]

REVIEWING THE SKILL

Write the criteria for evaluating evidence (see section on **Evaluation** in the "Guide to Critical Thinking," student text, page 3) on the board and have students copy it into their notebooks. You could also ask a volunteer to make a poster to remind students of the criteria (below).

EVALUATING EVIDENCE

Is there a source for the information?

If no, the information is unsupported and weakened.

If yes, evaluate it:

P — primary or secondary?

R — reason to lie or exaggerate?

O — other evidence to verify this evidence?

P — public or private?

This process of making posters for the classroom can be repeated for other skills and their criteria.

USING THE WORKSHEET

When the class has completed the role-play activity and the discussion, you can pass out Worksheet B (pp. 33–34) as an immediate follow-up on evaluating evidence. Tell the students they are going to practice what they have just learned about evaluating evidence.

Suggested Answers

- The jury was probably right in its guilty verdict.

Point out that making the historical judgment that Lucky stabbed John Jones is not the same as finding him guilty in court. In history, unlike in court, we do not have to prove something "beyond a reasonable doubt," but rather provide enough evidence to show that the person probably did it. In other words, we might say we think Lucky committed the murder, but should have been found "not guilty" in court. We do not presume innocence in history as we do in trials.

A. Statements are numbers 1–10, 12, and 15– 17.

B. Documents are numbers 14 and 18.

C. Objects are numbers 11 and 13.

- The evidence is evaluated as follows.

    P—Is the evidence primary?

    R—Does the person have a reason to lie?

    O—Is there other supporting evidence?

    P—Is the evidence private?

	4	7	10	11	14	17	18
P	no	yes	yes	yes	yes	no	no
R	yes	yes	no	no	no	no	no
O	no	yes	yes	yes	yes	yes	yes
P	no	no	no	yes	yes	yes	yes

- Since evidence 18 is private and seems to have no reason to lie, it is more reliable than evidence 4. Not foolproof; just more likely to be reliable.

Worksheet C: Sources and Evidence

Objectives

To identify sources
To evaluate evidence

Teaching Ideas
  USING THE WORKSHEET

Students must first determine if a source for the information is given. Then, if there is a source, they are to evaluate it according to the four questions explained in the Worksheet C handout.

Distribute copies of the worksheet and ask the students to complete as much as they can. Remind them that a longer explanation of evidence can be found on pages 2–4 in Unit 1 of their book.

When students have filled in as much of the sheet as they can, have them compare answers in groups of three. Finally, discuss the worksheet as a class.

Suggested Answers

1. Since the statement gives no source for the information, it cannot be further evaluated. Thus, the evidence is not well supported.

    [You will need to point out to some students that even though a specific figure ($15 million) is used, we do not know where the figure came from; no source is given.]

2. The scorebook is the source for the statistic. **P**—it is a primary source, since the scorekeeper had to be at the games; **R**—there is no reason for the scorebook (or scorekeeper) to lie about hits and times at bat (batting average); **O**—there is no other evidence given to support the claim that Kurt is a great hitter; **P**—it is a public statement. **Overall**, this would be considered a reliable source.

3. The three workers' statements at the public hearings are the source. **P**—the workers say they saw payoffs, so they are primary sources; **R**—the workers might have motives to lie or exaggerate if they do not like Mayor Pratt; **O**—the three workers verify each other; **P**—these are public statements. **Overall**, the fact that three people were willing to risk testifying about the corruption does carry some weight, although the evidence is not as reliable as that in problem 2.

4. There is no source given for the information, so it is not well supported.

Worksheet D: Evaluating Evidence — PROP

Objectives

To evaluate sources of evidence

Teaching Ideas
USING THE WORKSHEET

Pass out the worksheet. Ask the students to fill it in then discuss their answers as a class. If students are confused about any of the criteria, the following questions may help them clarify their evaluations.

QUESTIONS FOR DETERMINING EVIDENCE

- To determine if someone is a **primary source**, ask, "Was this person at the location when the event occurred, or was she talking about herself?"

- To determine if someone has a **reason to lie**, ask, "Did this person make him- or herself look good by the statement?" [Why would s/he lie to make him or herself look bad?]

- To determine if there is **other supporting evidence**, ask, "Who said this? Did any other people say the same thing?"

- To determine if the evidence is **public**, ask, "Did this person make the statement to influence anyone else? Does he or she think anyone other than the person spoken to would hear what was said?"

Suggested Answers

1. Yu-chi **P**—is a primary source; **R**—has a reason to lie; **O**—presents no supporting evidence; **P**—the statement is public, meant to influence his father. **Overall**, the evidence is not very reliable because of the reason to lie and the lack of supporting evidence.

2. Laura **P**—is a primary source about talking with Jill (but she was not at the scene of the baby-sitting); **R**—may have a reason to lie if she wants to protect Jill (we don't know); **O**—has supporting evidence provided by Connie's and Ellen's statements; **P**—the statement is public, meant to influence Bob. **Overall**, this is fairly good evidence.

3. Christie **P**—is a primary source; **R**—has no reason to lie, as her statement places the blame on herself; **O**—offers no supporting evidence; **P**—it is a public statement. **Overall**, Christie's evidence is strong. [Admitting she had done wrong is unlikely to be a lie, but it is possible—for example, if she had failed because she had skipped school, which might have gotten her into worse trouble.]

Worksheet E: Cause-and-Effect Reasoning

Objectives

To recognize cause-and-effect reasoning
To evaluate cause-and-effect reasoning

Teaching Ideas

INTRODUCING THE SKILL

Introduce cause-and-effect reasoning by telling the class that you, the teacher, just entered the emergency room with a terrible pain in your stomach. They are the doctors on duty. What would they ask? Set it up that you have been at the beach all day and left your ham and mayonnaise sandwich out in the hot sun.

Although some student may focus on what you ate and the likelihood of food poisoning early in the discussion, other students may later ask questions about appendicitis, medication, and alcohol. They are considering other possible causes for the problem. You could ask the class how they could test their hypothesis further to focus them on the connection between each proposed cause and effect. How could they check to be more certain it was food poisoning from the sandwich? (A blood test showing bacteria in the blood would show a connection).

REINFORCING THE SKILL

While these questions for evaluating cause-and-effect reasoning are being discussed, write them on the chalkboard. As with evaluating evidence, the students should be instructed to copy the questions into their notebooks and someone should make a poster to be put up in the classroom. For further discussion of this skill, refer students to the **Cause-and-Effect Reasoning** section of the "Guide to Critical Thinking" (pp. 5–7 in their text).

USING THE WORKSHEET

Once you have laid out the steps in evaluating cause-and-effect reasoning you can pass out Worksheet E for students to try for guided practice. When they have completed the worksheet, have them compare answers in small groups or in a whole-class discussion.

Suggested Answers

1.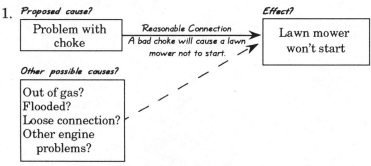

Overall, this is not very strong reasoning since other possible causes have not been ruled out.

Overall, this is very strong reasoning since other possible causes have been ruled out.

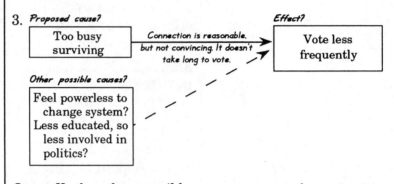

Overall, the other possible causes seem as important to the effect as the proposed cause. It is not a very strong argument.

Worksheet F: Comparison Arguments

Objectives

To introduce criteria for evaluating comparisons

Teaching Ideas

INTRODUCING THE SKILL

Have students do the introductory problem first. Make sure they write down their questions, then discuss the problem as a class.

After they have given their answers to the autocross problem, ask students what questions they ask to evaluate comparisons in general? (How are the two cases different?) If necessary, refer students to the section on **Comparisons** in the "Guide to Critical Thinking" (pp. 7–8 in the student text).

USING THE WORKSHEET

When students are ready to evaluate the comparison arguments, have them write their answers individually, then discuss the problems in small groups. Note to students that in Problem 3, since Candice is arguing that the radios are different, the students should focus on identifying similarities.

Suggested Answers

INTRODUCTORY PROBLEM

Some Autocross Race questions to ask:

1. What kind of car were you driving?

2. Was it the same course?

3. What were the weather conditions?

Emphasize to the students that they already know how to evaluate comparison arguments. They just showed it by the questions they asked.

COMPARISONS

1. Margarine substitute

   — Compared: butter and margarine

   — Possible differences: taste; amount or type of fat

   — Possible similarities: function in baking

   — Overall: They are similar enough to allow the cake to still come out as a cake, although there might be some difference in taste and texture. To demonstrate the similarities between butter and margarine, ask students what would happen if they substituted jelly for butter.

2. Statewide test

   — Compared: student performance on one test at Centralville and Evantown

— Possible differences:

a. The student body of the two schools might be very different. For example, students might vary in educational background, ethnic background, economic opportunities, or social class.

b. The test may have been given in different grades in the two schools.

c. The curriculum at Centralville might be more suited to the test.

d. Testing circumstances at the two schools may have differed; e.g., physical testing environment; attitudes of students toward test; school activities before or after test, etc.

—Possible similarities: All above items might be similar rather than different.

—Overall: Not enough information is given. If most or all of the above items are different, then the comparison is very weak.

3. Deluxe Radio

—Compared: deluxe and standard radio models

—Possible differences: Cost is the only known difference; number of stations and sound quality are implied differences.

—Possible similarities: We don't know if the standard radio can also do the things the deluxe model can do.

—Overall: Candice has not drawn a reasonable conclusion. She may be satisfied with the radio, but she has not shown that the extra $50 was worth it. If the standard radio plays all the stations she likes and has a clear sound, then Candice's money was not well spent. In this comparison, the possible similarities undermine the argument because Candice is arguing they are different and that the difference makes the extra money spent worthwhile.

Worksheet G: Understanding Comparisons

Objectives

To identify comparison reasoning
To evaluate comparison arguments

Teaching Ideas

Have students write their answers individually, then discuss and defend their answers in small groups. Or you can discuss answers as a class.

Suggested Answers

• Numbers **1** and **5** are comparisons. Other items may have comparisons implied in them, but the comparison is not a key part of the argument.

8. A	11. D	14. D
9. D	12. A	
10. D	13. A	

15. a. Compares John's taste in movies to mine.

    b. It's an alike comparison.

    c. Since John is different from me in some ways, his taste in movies is likely to be different from mine in some ways.

    d. If John's movie taste is different from mine in a way that's important for this movie, then it might be a poor comparison. For example, if John doesn't mind violence in movies but I do, and if this movie is violent, then the comparison argument is faulty.

16. a. Compares Wranglers' team record to Panthers' team record.

    b. It's a different comparison (claims that since they are different from each other in a particular way, they are different in other particular ways also).

    c. Additional information would be needed in the areas of number of games and opponents. They may be similar or different.

    d. The more similarities that are found between the two teams, the stronger the argument that the Wranglers' team is better.

17. a. Compares state university to private college.

    b. It's an alike comparison.

    c. Areas of possible comparison might include social life, facilities, library sources, cost, etc.

    d. Maybe other aspects of the private college are better. On the other hand, if the campus and professors are the most important considerations to Carrie, then this is a good comparison.

18. a. Compares the private college to public colleges. (The comparison is implicit in "extra money.")

    b. It is a difference comparison.

  c–d. Since the statement doesn't say that the soccer team and the professors are better than at other, less expensive schools, there is no basis for making the claim that the extra money was worth it.

Worksheet H: Evaluating Generalizations

Objectives

To recognize and evaluate generalizations

Teaching Ideas
  USING THE WORKSHEET

The first worksheet section focuses on evaluating generalization claims. A circle diagram is shown for the example problem. If students find such diagrams helpful, encourage them to draw their own for problems 1–3.

The second section of the worksheet focuses on how far given information may be generalized. There is room for reasonable disagreement on these questions, so try to avoid pushing for one right answer. Ask students for the reasons for their answers. Focus on the subgroups of the major group in the generalization.

You might want to have the class read over the section on generalizations in the "Guide to Critical Thinking." If not, you can refer them to that section if they need help.

Suggested Answers

1. a. The generalization is that most kids in the school watch more than 12 hours of television a week.

    b. Subgroups might include honors, average, or remedial students; those involved in extracurricular activities and those who aren't; students who have jobs and those who don't; students from various income levels; students of various home environments; and so forth.

    c. The sample is relatively small (30 out of 800, or about 4%).

    d. The sample may have most of the subgroups by random distribution, but since it is a specific class, it is an ability group.

    e. This isn't a great sample because the amount of homework generally affects how much television a student watches. If this is a remedial class, the number of hours watched probably is not the same as the number of hours watched by honors students.

2. a. The generalization is that all Italians belong to the Mafia.

    b. Subgroups include different intelligence levels; different levels of education, income, and occupation; different geographic locations; different family lives and background; and so forth.

c. The sample may be exceedingly small (this person may know one Italian who belongs to the Mafia), somewhat larger (the person may live in an Italian neighborhood and know many Italians), or nonexistent (the person may have heard that Italians belong to the Mafia). Even with the larger sample, however, it is very small compared to the millions of Italians in the world.

d. We don't know much about the sample, but we can say with reasonable assurance that not all the subgroups are represented well.

e. This is a poor generalization. It is a good example of a stereotype—a large, complex group of people being simplified to all having a particular characteristic.

3. a. The generalization is that the population of Mudville rose dramatically in the 1970s.

b. As far as we know, the sample covers everyone in the large group (Mudville).

c. The generalization is very strong, which tells us that census records are good sources.

4. Neither A nor D are reasonable extensions of the information in your sample since both contain nonpublic, nonsuburban, and nonsecondary schools. (Is homework a key to good grades in elementary schools?) B, although restricted to your own suburban district, is weak for one of the same reasons that A and D are weak: it includes elementary schools. C is the best of the given choices. It is restricted to public suburban high schools, although it does extend the sample generalization too far geographically.

5. D is the best choice since it is the only one that emphasizes both the mountains and a strong defense. A emphasizes only defense, and it is unclear how being large or small affects avoiding war (B and C).

6. A is the best choice. The students in your school may be different (for example, in terms of educational or cultural background) from those in other schools, which makes it difficult to extend the sample beyond your own school (B and C). The information you have says nothing about the type of music students do not like.

Worksheet I: Identifying Unstated Assumptions—1

Objectives

To recognize arguments based on assumptions
To identify assumptions made by others

Teaching Ideas

INTRODUCING THE SKILL

To encourage students to begin recognizing their own assumptions, give half the class statement 1 and the other half statement 2. Ask them to write an answer to the question. Don't say they have different statements.

1. "The Soviet Union gives a great deal of economic aid to India." Why do you think the Soviet Union does this?

2. "The United States gives a great deal of economic aid to India." Why do you think the United States does this?

When each student has written a response, list the various reasons on the chalkboard and ask the students to count the number of positive and negative motives attributed to each country. Were more positive motives given to the United States? If so, why?

Students may contend that the Soviet Union is an expansionist country which is trying to spread communism. The question "How do you know they are expansionist?" will force them to examine how they arrived at their belief. Similarly, "How do you know the United States is giving aid for humanitarian reasons?" will force them to question how they arrived at that belief. While it *may* be true that Soviet aid is self-serving and American aid is humanitarian, students should examine how they arrived at these beliefs. Did they have supporting evidence or did their frame of reference lead to the assumption?

USING THE WORKSHEET

It is probably better to start with this worksheet rather than Worksheet J. If students can identify the assumptions on this worksheet, then they probably do not need the more structured approach.

Suggested Answers

1. Your brother gets good grades in school because he studies. Your lower grades in school are due to lack of study (as opposed to other reasons).

2. Peter is the same age as (or older than) Marie.

3. You run faster than I do.

4. You don't have good writing skills.

5. I don't have other unexpected expenses. I'll be alive. I'll be able to drive.

6. Drinking is a way to enjoy life. Jim is too serious.

Worksheet J: Identifying Unstated Assumptions—2

Objectives

To provide a structured approach to identifying assumptions in arguments

Teaching Ideas

It is probably a good idea to start assumptions with Introductory Worksheet I. If students can identify the assumptions in that worksheet, then they may not need this more structured approach. You may also choose to use this step-by-step approach with only a few students.

If you do use this worksheet, have the students discuss problem 1 as a class before they go on. Give students time to do problem 2 individually, then discuss their answers. Repeat this procedure for problem 3.

Suggested Answers

2. Step 1: (Premise) "Because" Fred works for a station which does fine work...

   Step 2: (Conclusion) "Therefore," Fred is a good mechanic.

   Step 3: (Unique parts) works for a station which does fine work/good mechanic

   Step 4: (Assumption) "People" who work for a station which does fine mechanical work must be good mechanics.

3. Step 1: (Premise) "Because" Sequoia is in the band (and Leona isn't)...

   Step 2: (Conclusion) "Therefore," Sequoia is a better musician (than Leona).

   Step 3: (Unique parts) in the band/better musician

   Step 4: (Assumption) "People" who are in a band are better musicians (than those who aren't).

WORKSHEET A   The Bermuda Triangle

(1) The Bermuda Triangle—an area roughly from Bermuda, southwest to Florida, then east out into the Atlantic, and then northwest back to Bermuda—is one of the most dangerous and strange spots on earth. Beginning back in the 1600s and continuing to today, the number of ships lost in the Triangle is staggering. In recent years an average of about one hundred ships and many airplanes have been lost in the area each year. It is common knowledge among commercial pilots and ship captains that the Triangle is a dangerous place.

(2) What has happened to these boats and planes is especially mysterious, however, and that is what gives the area its name as the "Devil's Triangle." For example, a boat named the *Hollyhock* was off the coast of Florida when it suddenly lost radio contact with the coast. Later, it picked up California on the radio. Then it spotted land on its monitors where there was no land! The *Hollyhock* disappeared without a trace.

(3) Another boat, the *Witchcraft*, was at Buoy Number 7, only two miles off the coast of Miami, when the owner radioed to the Coast Guard for assistance because the boat was taking on water. He reassured the Coast Guard, however, that the boat was in no serious danger for it had built-in flotation chambers. When the Coast Guard arrived at Buoy Number 7, the *Witchcraft* had vanished.

(4) Airplanes, too, have had bizarre incidents. The *Star Tiger*, flying over the Devil's Triangle, suddenly lost all radio contact. No wreckage of the plane was ever found. In 1963 two KC-135 jet tankers disappeared three hundred miles southwest of Bermuda. What caused these planes to go down?

(5) Probably the most incredible incident concerned Training Flight 19, which took off from Fort Lauderdale, Florida, on December 5, 1945. Five Avenger aircraft took off that day on a regular Navy training flight. Pilot Cosner did not go on the flight. Why not? Commander Taylor also seemed hesitant. Did he have the same peculiar feeling as Cosner? The flight was routine at first, but then mysterious things started to happen. The pilots seemed confused and their instruments were doing weird things. The air base which had radio contact with the planes heard the pilots say, "Which way is west?" and the phrases "upside down" and "white water." The planes kept changing directions, almost flying in circles. Then—silence. A search plane was sent out and it, too, disappeared. The Navy has kept the incident quiet, and it hasn't denied the stories that authors have written about it.

(6) It is difficult to explain what happens in the Devil's Triangle. Some people believe there is a magnetic field which throws everything off. Others believe it has to do with the lost continent of Atlantis. Whatever the cause, it is worth thinking twice before traveling through this area—one of the strangest spots on our earth.

©1991 MIDWEST PUBLICATIONS/CRITICAL THINKING PRESS & SOFTWARE, P.O. BOX 448, PACIFIC GROVE, CA 93950

Relevant Information on the Bermuda Triangle

1. The *Star Tiger*'s flight was at night in poor weather.

2. It is not unheard of, although it is infrequent, for boats out in the ocean to pick up distant areas on the radio.

3. Rain clouds can sometimes look like land on radar.

4. The *Witchcraft* was out in bad weather.

5. Coast Guard reports make no mention of the *Witchcraft* being near Buoy Number 7. An author estimated the location by comparing several reports.

6. It would have taken the Coast Guard about twenty minutes to get from their station to where the *Witchcraft* was.

7. In twenty minutes a boat in calm seas can drift about one mile.

8. It is extremely difficult to find the wreckage of a plane or boat in the ocean, even on a clear day.

9. Debris found in one spot in the ocean contained the serial numbers of both KC-135 jet tankers. Some observers say this indicates that the two planes collided in the air.

10. The editor of *Aviation Week* stated that, based on a statistical analysis of the number of accidents in an area compared with the number of flights in that area, the Bermuda Triangle is one of the safest spots in the world. It is a popular area with pilots.

11. An Avenger aircraft will sink into the ocean roughly forty-five seconds after splashing down.

12. Two of the men who were in the radio tower in Fort Lauderdale at the time of Training Flight 19 do not recall the Avenger pilots saying "Which way is west?" or "upside down" or "white water." These two men say the planes were definitely lost.

13. Commander Taylor of Training Flight 19 radioed, "If we fly north, then east, we'll get home." He also mentioned being over the Keys (islands). He may have thought he was over the Florida Keys, when actually he was over the Grand Keys in the Atlantic. His proposed course of "north, then east" would have taken the planes toward the middle of the Atlantic.

14. At the time that radio contact was lost with the plane sent to search for Training Flight 19, people on the coast saw what looked like an explosion near the search plane's last-reported location.

15. Out of 10,000 distress calls made to the Coast Guard in that area, about 100 ships are lost in the Bermuda Triangle each year.

16. According to the Coast Guard, many pleasure boat owners don't know what they're doing in the ocean. For example, when the Coast Guard told one owner to plot a course toward an island, the owner said he couldn't find it on his map. The Coast Guard asked him what map he was using, and he said he was looking at the world atlas.

17. Each author who writes about the Bermuda Triangle describes a triangle of a different size and shape from the other authors.

18. The author of this Bermuda Triangle article writes books on popular subjects, such as mysterious and bizarre phenomena.

WORKSHEET B   Evaluating Evidence

Background

You, as a historian, are trying to decide who stabbed John Jones in 1940 in the corridor at your school. You have gathered the following information (evidence) about the case.

Relevant Information

A.   The report on the police investigation into the death of John Jones says:
1.   The police concluded that he was murdered by stab wounds.
2.   The police had three suspects: 1) Kid Kelly, 2) Slim Stowell, and 3) Lucky Levin. All three were in the corridor within ten feet of Jones when he was murdered.
3.   Police thought they had enough evidence to prosecute Lucky Levin.

B.   Lucky Levin was tried for the alleged murder of John Jones. In the trial:
4.   Lucky's girlfriend said he was a good person and would never kill anyone.
5.   A teacher testified he opened the door of his room and entered the corridor as soon as he heard John Jones scream. No one could have moved, and no one was moving when he looked into the corridor. Jones was lying on the floor while Lucky, Kid, and Slim were standing within ten feet, looking at him. Lucky was closest to Jones.
6.   Kid testified that he didn't do it, but he was looking the other way so he doesn't know whether Lucky or Slim did it.
7.   Slim testified that he didn't do it, Lucky did it.
8.   Lucky testified that he didn't do it, Slim did it.
9.   Witness A, who didn't know any of the men, said he heard Jones say, "No, Lucky, no" right before the murder.
10.   Witness B, who was 35 feet away and who didn't know any of the men, said he saw Lucky stab Jones.
11.   The knife was shown to have Lucky's, and only Lucky's, fingerprints on it.
12.   According to Kid, both Lucky and Slim had knives with them on the day of the death.
13.   The police found a knife on Slim at the scene of the murder, as well as the knife in Jones. No other weapons were found.
14.   An IOU note produced at the trial showed that Jones owed Lucky $300, which had been due to be paid three days before the murder.
15.   Witness C testified that Slim did not like Jones.
16.   Witness D, 50 feet away, testified that she saw Lucky stab Jones.
17.   Witness E, in another part of the building and not within sight of the murder scene, says he's sure Lucky killed Jones.
18.   At the trial, a letter from Lucky's girlfriend to her mother was introduced as evidence. The letter said that Lucky hated John Jones.

C.   The jury found Lucky guilty of murder.

Evaluate the Evidence

 As a historian, do you think the jury was right in its verdict? Why do you think so?

 Give one example from the Relevant Information section on page 33 for each type of evidence listed below. Write the number of the evidence on the line provided.

     _____A. Statements by witnesses

     _____B. Documents (written information)

     _____C. Objects

 Evaluate (judge) the following evidence selected from the Relevant Information. Use the **PROP** factors (criteria) from the section on **Evidence** in the "Guide to Critical Thinking" (pp. 2–4).

Factor #	4	7	10	11	14	17	18
P							
R							
O							
P							

 Compare the reliability of evidence 4 and evidence 18. Which is more reliable? Explain your answer.

WORKSHEET C   Sources and Evidence

Whenever you see information used in support of an argument you should ask certain questions, the first and most important being, "Does the information have a source given?"

A *source* is the person, place, or written document the information came from. If there is no given source, the information cannot be evaluated and should not be accepted as reliable.

If the information does give a source, you can evaluate its reliability by asking a number of questions, four of which are given here. For further help, see the section on **Evidence** in the "Guide to Critical Thinking."

Criteria for Evaluating Evidence

P   Is it a **primary** (more reliable) or secondary (less reliable) source?

R   Does the person giving the evidence have any **reason to lie** (less reliable)?

O   Is there **other evidence** which supports or verifies what this evidence says (more reliable) or is this the only evidence presented on the topic (less reliable)?

P   Is it a public (less reliable) or **private** (more reliable) statement? It is public if the person giving it knew other people would read or see it.

 Evaluate each of the following arguments using the above questions.

1. The city government under Mayor Elwell was very corrupt. Over $15 million was stolen in only five years.

    Is there a source given for any information in this argument? _____
    If not, the claim of corruption is not well supported by evidence.
    If yes, evaluate the evidence and explain your evaluation.

    P

    R

    O

    P

---

2.   Kurt is a great hitter. The statistics from last season's scorebook show he hit .457, a very high average.

     Is there a source given for any information in this argument? _____

     If not, the argument is not well supported. If yes, evaluate it.

     P

     R

     O

     P

3.   The city government under Mayor Pratt was very corrupt. Three city workers stated in public hearings that they each had seen money paid to city officials for special favors.

     Is there a source given for any information in this argument? _____

     If not, the argument is not well supported. If yes, evaluate it.

     P

     R

     O

     P

4.   Kelley is a great hitter. She can hit the fast ball and the curve.

     Is there a source given for any information in this argument? _____

     If not, the argument is not well supported. If yes, evaluate it.

     P

     R

     O

     P

WORKSHEET D   Evaluating Evidence — PROP

You will recall that the first question you should ask about information (evidence) is whether or not a source is given. Each argument on this worksheet names the source, or the person who said it. For further explanation see the section on **Evidence** in the "Guide to Critical Thinking."

Criteria for Evaluating Evidence

P   Is it a **primary** (more reliable) or secondary (less reliable) source?

R   Does the person giving the evidence have any **reason to lie** (less reliable)?

O   Is there **other evidence** which supports or verifies what this evidence says (more reliable) or is this the only evidence presented on the topic (less reliable)?

P   Is it a public (less reliable) or **private** (more reliable) statement? It is public if the person giving it knew other people would read or see it.

 Evaluate each of the following situations according to the four criteria given below.

1.   Yu-chi tells his father it was not his fault that he got detention. He said that the teacher thought he was talking during class, but he wasn't.

Evaluate Yu-chi's evidence according to the four criteria.

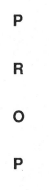

       P

       R

       O

       P

Overall, how reliable is Yu-chi's evidence?

2. Bob is angry because he thinks his girlfriend, Jill, went out with Larry on Friday. Laura, Connie, and Ellen all told Bob that they had talked with Jill on the phone most of the night on Friday while she was baby-sitting, so she couldn't have gone out with Larry.

   Evaluate Laura's evidence according to the four criteria.

   P

   R

   O

   P

   Overall, how reliable is Laura's evidence?

3. Christie tells her parents she failed English because she didn't study. She says she has no one to blame but herself and has to admit she deserves to be grounded.

   Evaluate Christie's evidence about why she failed.

   P

   R

   O

   P

   Overall, how reliable is Christie's evidence?

WORKSHEET E Cause-and-Effect Reasoning

When someone proposes a cause for some situation or event, he or she is using cause-and-effect reasoning. Following these steps will help you evaluate such arguments.

EVALUATING CAUSE-AND-EFFECT REASONING

1. Decide which is the cause and which is the effect.

2. See if the person explains how the cause led to the effect. If the person doesn't explain, we should ask if there is a reasonable connection between the cause and the effect.

3. Ask if there are other possible causes for this effect. Has this person eliminated these other possible causes?

 Using a diagram like the one shown after the first problem will help you follow these steps when evaluating cause-and-effect reasoning. Draw your own diagrams for the other problems.

1. The repairman says that Mark's lawn mower won't start because of a problem with the choke, which will cost $25.00 to fix.

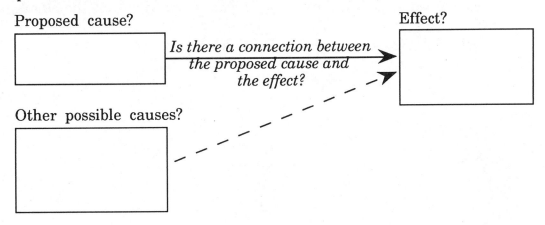

Overall, how strong is the repairman's cause-and-effect reasoning?

2. Mr. Alberti insulated his house before this winter started. The average temperature this winter has been about the same as last winter, and Mr. Alberti has kept the thermostat at the same settings both winters. So far, he has used 40% fewer gallons of oil than he had at this time last winter. He thinks the insulation has been very effective in saving heating oil.

   Analyze Mr. Alberti's cause-and-effect thinking. Use a diagram.

   Overall, how strong is the argument?

3. Low-income people tend to vote less frequently than high-income people because poorer people are so busy trying to survive that they don't take time to vote.

   Draw a diagram and analyze this thinking.

   Overall, how strong is the argument?

WORKSHEET F   Comparison Arguments

Introductory Problem

> Suppose you drove in an autocross race at the North Shore Shopping Center parking lot a month ago. ("Autocross" is a race over a winding course set up with cone markers. Cars race one at a time and are clocked as they run the course.) You drove your 1952 Plymouth, and your time was 36.8 seconds. Now, suppose Harry told you that last Sunday he was in an autocross and his time was 28.2 seconds. He says this proves he is a better driver than you are.

Write three questions that you would want to ask Harry.

1.

2.

3.

Evaluating Comparison Arguments

A comparison argument reasons that since two cases are similar in some respects they will also be similar in another way. You can tell from the questions you wrote above that the key to deciding the strength of a comparison argument is asking, "How are the two cases different?" Refer to the section on **Comparison Reasoning** in the "Guide to Critical Thinking" (Unit 1) if you need more help.

 Using the given questions, evaluate each of the following comparison arguments.

1. You are baking a cake and the recipe calls for 5 teaspoons of butter. You have no butter, so you reason that if you substitute 5 teaspoons of margarine the cake will still turn out fine.

    a.   What two items are being compared?

    b.   How are they different?

    c.   How are they alike?

    d.   Overall, how strong is this comparison argument?

2. The average score on the state-wide test was 12 points higher at Centralville High than it was at Evantown High. It is clear from these scores that the teachers at Centralville are doing a better job of teaching.

   a. What two items are being compared?

   b. How are they different?

   c. How are they alike?

   d. Overall, how strong is this comparison argument?

3. Candice paid $50 more to get the deluxe model when she bought her radio. She thinks the money was well spent because the radio gets all the stations she likes and the sound is very clear.

   a. What two items are being compared?

   b. How are they different?

   c. How are they alike?

   d. Overall, how strong is this comparison argument?

WORKSHEET G   Understanding Comparisons

For help, refer to the section about **Comparisons** in the "Guide to Critical Thinking."

Identifying Comparisons

 Put a "C" on the line in front of each of the following arguments or claims that use comparison reasoning.

_____ 1.   Jean felt the suede jacket was worth the extra money.

_____ 2.   Benji has been a great dog. He's very obedient and he doesn't bark much.

_____ 3.   Fred used his new equipment the last time he climbed.

_____ 4.   I decided to read *A Tale of Two Cities* because, although it is long, it is an excellent story.

_____ 5.   You should buy alkaline batteries; they last longer than regular ones.

_____ 6.   Tom and Pat helped us out a lot when we had to fix the house. They are good neighbors.

_____ 7.   Tomika hit the other car when she backed up in the parking lot.

Categorizing Comparisons

Mark each of the following arguments. Put an **S** in front of arguments which claim that the two cases are basically similar. Put a **D** in front of arguments which claim that the two cases are basically different. Remember, better/worse comparisons emphasize differences.

_____ 8.   You gave Mari $5.00 for her work, so you should give me $5.00 for my work, too.

_____ 9.   Since our team has won more games this year than last, we must have improved.

_____ 10.   Rachel is the right player to guard their scorer. Julie just isn't as good on defense.

_____ 11.   The new deluxe sedan costs a little more but it's well worth it. It has cruise control and an engine.

_____ 12.   I beat George at chess last time, so I'm sure I will again.

_____ 13.   Jim has never charged us more than $50.00 for a repair in the past, so he surely won't charge us too much this time.

_____ 14.   I'm sticking with Toni because she's a better computer programmer than Geoffrey is.

Analyzing and Evaluating Comparisons

 Each of the following problems presents a comparison argument for you to analyze and evaluate. The **Example** is done for you.

Example:

"I jumped 5'6" in the last meet, so I should jump at least 5'6" today.

    a.   What are the two cases or characteristics being compared?

        Case A: [the speaker's jumping ability at the last meet]

        Case B: [the speaker's jumping ability today]

    b.   Is this an alike or different comparison?

        [Alike]

    c.   What similarities or differences are there between the two cases?

        [Similarities: same goal in same event]

        [Differences: the jumper's health or condition may be different today; weather, jumping conditions, or training time may differ]

    d.   How strong is the comparison?

        [It's reasonable, but it should take into account the possible differences. For example, if the jumper claimed to be in better condition now and the weather is favorable, then the conclusion would be stronger.]

15.   "My best friend, John, liked the movie, so I bet I'll like it too."

    a.   What are the two cases or characteristics being compared? Be precise!

        Case A:

        Case B:

    b.   Is this an alike or different comparison?

    c.   What similarities or differences are there between the two cases?

    d.   How strong is the comparison?

16.   "The Wranglers have a better team than the Panthers. The Wranglers have more wins and fewer losses."

    a.   What are the two cases or characteristics being compared?

        Case A:

        Case B:

    b.   Is this an alike or different comparison?

c. What similarities or differences are there between the two cases?

d. How strong is the comparison?

17. Carrie decided that the state university is just as good as the private college in her area. The campus and the professors at the state university are as good as those at the private college.
a. What are the two cases or characteristics being compared?
Case A:

Case B:

b. Is this an alike or different comparison?

c. What similarities or differences are there between the two cases?

d. How strong is the comparison?

18. Roger decides that the extra money he spends to attend the private college is well worth it. The soccer team is excellent at the private college, as are the professors.
a. What are the two cases or characteristics being compared?
Case A:

Case B:

b. Is this an alike or different comparison?

c. What similarities or differences are there between the two cases?

d. How strong is the comparison?

WORKSHEET H   Evaluating Generalizations

If you need help, refer to the definition and examples of **Generalization** in the "Guide to Critical Thinking." Remember that a circle diagram is useful to help visualize generalizations as an analysis aid. An example is done for you.

Example:

"Most American adults would like to own their own homes. Just last month a survey of 1232 students at five hundred colleges around the country showed that 62% of those students who responded want to own their own home."

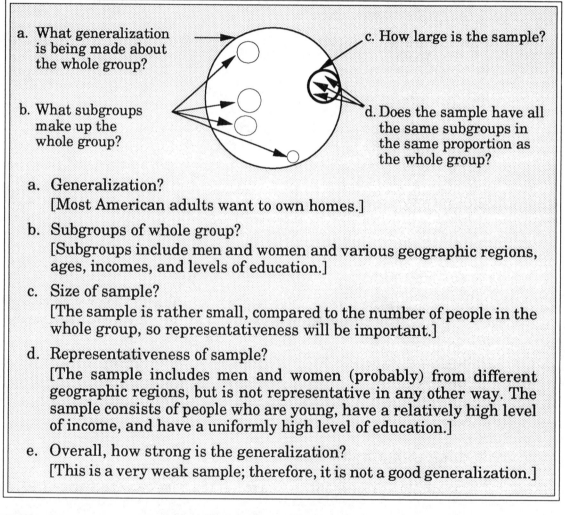

a. What generalization is being made about the whole group?

b. What subgroups make up the whole group?

c. How large is the sample?

d. Does the sample have all the same subgroups in the same proportion as the whole group?

a. Generalization?
[Most American adults want to own homes.]

b. Subgroups of whole group?
[Subgroups include men and women and various geographic regions, ages, incomes, and levels of education.]

c. Size of sample?
[The sample is rather small, compared to the number of people in the whole group, so representativeness will be important.]

d. Representativeness of sample?
[The sample includes men and women (probably) from different geographic regions, but is not representative in any other way. The sample consists of people who are young, have a relatively high level of income, and have a uniformly high level of education.]

e. Overall, how strong is the generalization?
[This is a very weak sample; therefore, it is not a good generalization.]

 Evaluate the following generalizations. Draw a circle graph and use the given questions to help with your evaluation.

1. "Most students in this high school [800 students] watch more than twelve hours of television a week. We took a poll in my social studies class, and twenty out of the thirty students said they watch more than twelve hours a week." [This school has honors, average, and remedial classes.]

a. Generalization?

b. Subgroups of whole group?

c. Size of sample?

d. Representativeness of sample?

e. Strength of generalization?

2. "I wouldn't hire an Italian if I were you. They all belong to the Mafia. Pretty soon you'll start having problems."

a. Generalization?

b. Subgroups of whole group?

c. Size of sample?

d. Representativeness of sample?

e. Strength of generalization?

3. "The 1980 census [a survey of every household in the country] showed that the population of Mudville rose dramatically during the 1970s."

a. Generalization?

b. Subgroups of whole group?

c. Size of sample?

d. Representativeness of sample?

e. Strength of generalization?

Write the letter of the most reasonable generalization on the line in front of each item. Explain your choice in the space provided.

_____4.   Suppose you found that in your public, suburban high school, those students who do more homework also get better grades. Which of the following is the best generalization to make from this information?

    A.   In your state, students who do more homework get better grades.

    B.   In your school district, students who do more homework get better grades.

    C.   In public, suburban high schools in the United States, students who do more homework get better grades.

    D.   Students who do more homework get better grades.

Explain your choice.

_____5.   Suppose you knew that Switzerland, which is a small, mountainous country, has used a strong defense (large military) to successfully avoid war. Which of the following is the best generalization to make from this information?

    A.   A large military is the key to avoiding war.

    B.   Small countries can use a strong defense to avoid war.

    C.   Large countries can use a strong defense to avoid war.

    D.   Mountainous countries can avoid war through building a strong defense.

Explain your choice.

_____6.   You know that 75% of the kids in your ninth-grade homeroom like rock music best. Which of the following is the best generalization to make from this information?

    A.   Most ninth-graders in your school like rock music best.

    B.   Anywhere you go in the country, you'll find that most teenagers like rock music best.

    C.   All ninth-grade students like rock music best.

    D.   Few ninth-grade students in your school like classical music.

Explain your choice.

WORKSHEET I   Identifying Unstated Assumptions — 1

What are the unstated assumptions in each of the following arguments? If you need help, look at the section on **Assumptions** in the "Guide to Critical Thinking."

1. "Why can't you study like your brother? He gets all A's in school."

2. "Beth is older than Peter, so she must be older than Marie also."

3. "Even if I have a head start running to the beach, you'll get there first."

4. "Are you sure you want to apply for that job? It requires someone with good writing skills."

5. "When I get my raise, I'm going to buy a new car."

6. "Jim, why don't you come drinking with us? You've got to learn to relax and enjoy life."

WORSHEET J   Identifying Unstated Assumptions — 2

This four-step approach is one method for identifying unstated assumptions.

Step 1	Write out the premise. (The premise is the part of an argument that tells "why" something is true. Look for the place to put "because." What follows is the premise.)
Step 2	Find and write out the conclusion of the argument. (Look for the place to put "therefore." What follows it is the conclusion.)
Step 3	Find the unique part of the conclusion (the part that doesn't appear in the premise) and the unique part of the premise (the part that doesn't appear in the conclusion.)
Step 4	Combine the two unique parts in a sentence that starts with a general word, such as people, wars, or countries. This sentence is the unstated assumption.

Q Try the four-step approach on the following claims. If you need help, look at the section on **Assumptions** in the "Guide to Critical Thinking." The first one is done for you as an example.

1. "Roger is not a football player since he weighs only 130 pounds."
   Step 1:   "Because" he weighs only 130 pounds. (Premise)
   Step 2:   "Therefore" Roger is not a football player. (Conclusion)
   Step 3:   ...weighs only 130 pounds (P)/...not a football player (C)
   Step 4:   "People" who weigh only 130 pounds are not football players.

2. Fred is definitely a good mechanic. He works for the service station on Main Street which is known for its fine mechanical work.
   Step 1:

   Step 2:

   Step 3:

   Step 4:

3. Sequoia is in the band and Leona isn't, so Sequoia must be a better musician.
   Step 1:

   Step 2:

   Step 3:

   Step 4:

WORKSHEET K   Analyzing Historical Films

When watching a film or video interpretation of any event, consider using the following (**PIPER**) model of analysis.

P	Point of View?
I	Inferences?
P	Persuasive Techniques?
E	Evidence?
R	Relevant Information?

Use this worksheet to help you analyze historical films you watch.

1. Name of film:

2. Main point of the film:

3. **P**   What is the **point of view** of the film? Was it overly favorable or critical of a particular group or individual?

4. **I**   What **inferences** were made in the film? Were there parts of the film that the filmmakers must have made up because they couldn't have known this from the available evidence?

5. **P**   What techniques are used in the film to **persuade** the audience to the filmmaker's point of view? Note camera angle, music, character portrayal, etc.

6. **E**   What **evidence** is included to support the point of view put forth in the film? What is the source of that evidence? How strong is it?

7. **R**   What **relevant information** do I know? Does it contradict or support the story presented in the film?

8. Overall, how strong are the historical arguments in this film? Is it historically accurate?

WORKSHEET L   Analyzing Historical Interpretations
Lesson _____   Interpretation _____

 Answer the following questions on each interpretation.

1.   What is the main idea of this interpretation?

2.   List two or three key points the author(s) use(s) to support the main idea, write any evidence given to support the point, and evaluate the evidence according to the **PROP** questions.

Key Point	Evidence that supports the point	Evaluation of Evidence
1		
2		

3.   Identify and analyze one cause-and-effect argument the interpretation makes. Fill in the cause and the effect first, then complete the diagram.

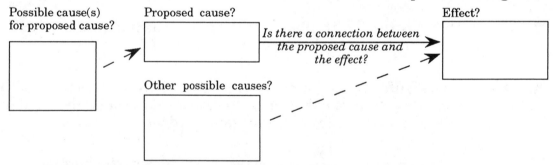

Overall, how strong is this cause-and-effect reasoning?

4.   Analyze any other aspect of the argument presented in the interpretation. For example, evaluate a generalization, comparison, or proof argument; identify an unstated assumption; note vague or emotional words that need to be defined more clearly by the author.

5.   If **Relevant Information** is provided, does any of the given information affect this interpretation? If so, identify the specific information by number(s) and state the effect(s) of each on the interpretation.

6.   What is your overall judgment of the interpretation? Identify its strengths and weaknesses.

UNIT 2
RECONSTRUCTION

Lesson 1: Identifying Sources

Objectives

To distinguish between supported and unsupported claims
To recognize sources of information

Teaching Ideas

This is a basic lesson to introduce students to the concept of asking for sources of information. Have students fill in the worksheet and discuss their answers in small groups. Then discuss the worksheet as a class by having a student give an answer to a question and asking if everyone agrees with the answer given. Have students explain why they agree or disagree.

Suggested Answers

1. S   The CBS poll is the source.
2. N
3. S   The Union lieutenant is the source.
4. N
5. N   Some people might argue that the Black Codes (the laws) are the source.
6. N
7. N
8. S   The source is the report cited in the endnote. Point out the use of endnotes to cite sources.

Lesson 2: Evaluating Sources

Objectives

To evaluate evidence according to specific criteria

Teaching Ideas

This basic lesson provides additional guidance for students who may have difficulty determining when a source is primary or when a person has a reason to lie.

Point out that having a "reason to lie" does not necessarily mean the source is lying; it just means you cannot accept what the source says without questioning it. Ask students to give reasons for their answer choice.

Suggested Answers

1. P

2. S   The publishing date shows that Boorstin was not there.

3. S?   If the newspaper did not have a reporter in the South it is a secondary source.

4. P   Lincoln is a primary source for his own policies.

5. P   The photograph gives us a first-hand view of the people.

6. N

7. R

8. N

9. N   It is hard to know why a historian, long after an event, would consciously lie about it, though historians like other people have unconscious biases.

10. R   The artist may be favorable toward blacks voting. The artist chose to show them smiling.

11. (#2) Corroborating evidence might be found in the *Congressional Record*, in speeches that Stevens made, in the records of other members of the House, or in the writings of his family and friends.

12. (#7) Corroborating evidence could be found in state records, in trials and investigations of Republican officials, and in newspaper accounts of corruption.

Lesson 3: Evaluating Evidence about Reconstruction

Objective

To apply criteria when evaluating historical evidence

Teaching Ideas

This is a more difficult lesson on evaluating evidence (or sources of information) than Lesson 2. If you use this lesson without using Lesson 2, students may learn criteria for evaluating evidence more quickly, but some students may be confused about some criteria. Lesson 2 may be helpful for those students.

PREPARATION

You might want to focus on the four main criteria for evidence evaluation (explained in the **Evidence** section of the "Guide to Critical Thinking" unit in the student book and in Introductory Worksheets B, C, and D in the teacher's guide).

EXTENDING ACTIVITY

After the class discusses student answers, ask students how they might further check on these pieces of evidence. Emphasize verification processes, especially those using primary sources. Some students might wish to do verification research on the topics using available resources.

Suggested Answers

1. [Jose]

STRENGTHS

• Primary source

WEAKNESSES

• Reason to lie
• No supporting evidence

2. [*Star*]

STRENGTHS

?

WEAKNESSES

• Secondary source
• No supporting evidence
• It has a reason to exaggerate—bizarre stories sell newspapers.
• Its reputation for reliability is not too strong.

3. [W. Beverly Nash]

STRENGTHS

• Primary source
• He had no reason to lie about accepting the bribe.
• The story could have been checked with Senator Leslie.

WEAKNESSES | • He had a reason to lie when he said it did not influence his vote.

4. [Governor Chamberlain]

STRENGTHS | • Primary source

WEAKNESSES | • Public statement—he was trying to influence people.
• Reason to lie to get reelected
• No supporting evidence of the corruption before he was governor

5. [Bernard Weisberger]

STRENGTHS | • No reason to lie

WEAKNESSES | • Secondary source
• No supporting evidence

Lesson 4: Recognizing and Assessing Cause-and-Effect Reasoning

Objectives

To identify cause-and-effect reasoning
To assess the strength of cause-and-effect relationships
To encourage students to think of alternative causes

Teaching Ideas

This is a basic lesson on cause-and-effect reasoning. Have students do the first problem in each section (1 and 6), then discuss their answers before they proceed with the other problems in the section.

Suggested Answers

1. C   Cause—missed the bus; effect—late for school

2. N

3. C   Cause—United States increasing military defenses; effect—Soviets negotiate arms reduction

4. C   Cause—Lincoln assassinated; effect—no chance for compromise with South

5. N

6. This argument greatly oversimplifies the causes for drug abuse. Plus, the speaker does not explain the connection between the cause and the effect. How does values-free education lead to drug abuse? There may be a connection, but since it is not clear, the author should explain it.

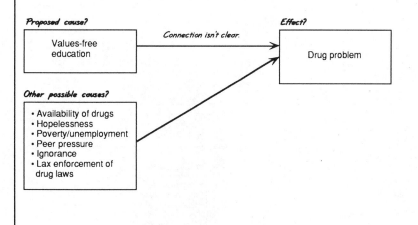

7. Again, this person oversimplifies a complex problem. Nevertheless, this cause makes sense and may be the

main cause. There would have to be some evidence to establish it as the main cause.

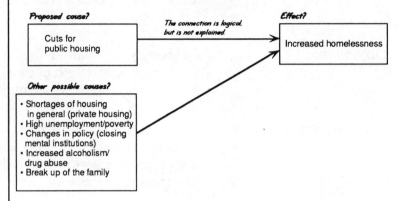

Proposed cause?

Cuts for public housing

The connection is logical, but is not explained.

Effect?

Increased homelessness

Other possible causes?

• Shortages of housing in general (private housing)
• High unemployment/poverty
• Changes in policy (closing mental institutions)
• Increased alcoholism/ drug abuse
• Break up of the family

8. This argument makes sense in that the Reconstruction Act would probably have caused resentment. It overlooks other causes of racism, however, such as slavery and a history of racism. In fact, injustices resulting from racism may actually have caused passage of the Reconstruction Act to protect blacks.

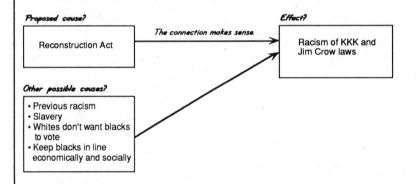

Proposed cause?

Reconstruction Act

The connection makes sense.

Effect?

Racism of KKK and Jim Crow laws

Other possible causes?

• Previous racism
• Slavery
• Whites don't want blacks to vote
• Keep blacks in line economically and socially

9. The connection is explained well, but the Republicans might have won the election for other reasons.

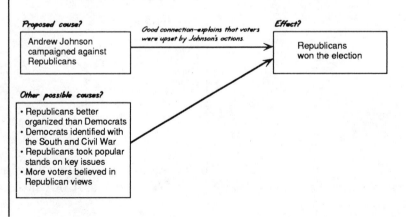

Proposed cause?

Andrew Johnson campaigned against Republicans

Good connection—explains that voters were upset by Johnson's actions.

Effect?

Republicans won the election

Other possible causes?

• Republicans better organized than Democrats
• Democrats identified with the South and Civil War
• Republicans took popular stands on key issues
• More voters believed in Republican views

Lesson 5: Identifying and Evaluating Generalizations

Objectives

To identify generalizations
To evaluate generalizations

Teaching Ideas

Before students begin this worksheet, ask them to define a generalization and to explain how they might evaluate one. You may want to have them read or review the section on **Generalizations** in the "Guide to Critical Thinking," pages 9–10, and review the introductory worksheet (Worksheet H, p. 46 in this Teacher's Guide) on this type of reasoning.

Students may need to be familiar with Reconstruction in order to answer question 9, but explaining the situation with the carpetbaggers might be enough.

This lesson is good preparation for Lesson 7 as the interpretations of Reconstruction in that lesson include a number of generalizations.

The first part of the worksheet (Questions 1–7) should be relatively easy. Begin the second section by having students answer question 8 and discuss it as a class, or by going over how to answer it as a class. Have students do the other two questions on their own.

Suggested Answers

1–7. Numbers 2, 5, 6, and 7 are generalizations. Note that each contains a plural noun.

  8. [Voters in 1866 Election]

    a. The generalization is that most voters disagreed with President Johnson.

    b. Subgroups might include males of various ages, levels of wealth, geographic location, occupation, education, racial groups, ethnic groups, and religions.

    c. The sample is of the whole voting group, since the vote itself records the choices of all the voters.

    d. Since the sample is complete, it covers all the subgroups.

    e. This is a very strong generalization about how the people voted.

9. [Carpetbaggers]

  a. The generalization is that carpetbaggers came to the South for political power and financial gain.

  b. Subgroups would include the various occupations of people who came to the South—Civil War veterans, teachers, Freedmen's Bureau agents, missionaries, investors, lawyers, etc. It would also include various ages and males and females.

  c. It is not clear what sample was taken. Perhaps no sampling was done. The simplicity of the generalization seems to show that a careful sample was not done.

  d. If a careful sample was not done then it does not have all the same subgroups; it is not representative of the carpetbaggers.

  e. This looks like a weak generalization. Some historians believe most carpetbaggers were Civil War veterans, missionaries, and female teachers. It is unlikely that missionaries and female teachers came South for political power and financial gain.

10. [Southerners and the Ku Klux Klan]

It is likely that no sample was taken. Nevertheless, the fact that the Ku Klux Klan could perform acts of violence for ten or more years does show that the general white population did not take strong action to stop it. Some individuals probably tried to stop it but not enough to have an effect for many years.

Lesson 6: How Corrupt Were Reconstruction Governments?

Objectives

To identify the main idea
To evaluate evidence
To evaluate cause and effect
To evaluate generalizations
To identify unstated assumptions

Teaching Ideas

This lesson focuses only on the question of corruption in the Republican governments in the South. Lesson 7 is more general but also hits this issue. There is no need to do this lesson if you do Lesson 7.

Have students read the introduction and question them to make sure they understand the overall situation and the issue in this lesson.

One way to continue is to have students read the two viewpoints and discuss in small groups the question for the lesson: "How corrupt were Reconstruction governments?" Then have each group give its opinion. A second way to proceed is to use the same sequence but have students answer the questions on the worksheets (pp. 31–33). This second approach will provide more structure but will take longer to discuss. You can shorten the lesson by having students answer only selected questions. Note questions 6 and 12 which focus students on the historians' world views.

Suggested Answers
HISTORIAN A

1. Main idea of Historian A—Republican governments were imposed on the South for the wrong reasons, were corrupt, and hurt the South.

2. Assumptions

  a. Paragraph 3—People who do not help get rights for blacks in their own area could not really be interested in rights for blacks in another area. (Radicals may have tried to get rights in Northern states but were outvoted. This argument involves the fallacy of composition (p. 10): the whole (the North) does not represent the part (the Radicals).)

  b. Paragraph 5, first sentence—Someone who makes an $8,000 a year salary but ends up with $100,000 is corrupt. (There might be other ways to make the money, but it does look suspicious.)

3. Evaluate a piece of evidence

   Endnote 1—Primary source, no reason to lie, unconscious prejudice against blacks, no supporting evidence of voting problems.

4. Evaluate the reasoning in:

   a. Paragraph 1—Generalizations about carpetbaggers and scalawags—All of the carpetbaggers and scalawags were not, undoubtedly, out for power and plunder. This argument stereotypes them (p. 10).

   b. Paragraphs 4 and 5—Generalization about corruption supported by the examples given—The question is whether the examples are representative of corruption in general. We don't know this from this argument.

   c. Paragraph 6—Cause and effect—The other possible causes for resentment and violence make this a weak argument.

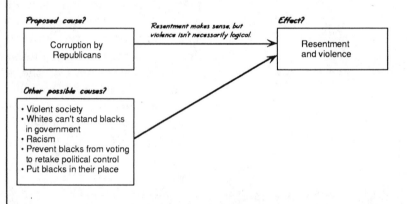

5. Words which make a value judgement—Plunged, misgovernment, plundering, and beyond belief all convey negative judgments.

6. D and A and possibly B. Have students explain their answers.

HISTORIAN B

7. Main idea of Historian B—Reconstruction governments in the South were not that corrupt and made significant achievements.

8. Assumption in Paragraph 6, first and second sentences—Governments must play a big part in physical reconstruction after a war.

9. Evaluate a piece of evidence:

   Endnote 1—Secondary, no reason to lie, no other supporting evidence. (Unfortunately, no sources are given for the many statistics used in the argument.)

10. Evaluate the reasoning in:

a. Paragraph 2, first and second sentences—This is a generalization about carpetbaggers that is much stronger than Historian A's (see suggested answer 4a) since it includes subgroups (see the section on **Generalizations** on pp. 9–10). We do not know, however, how large or representative a sample was taken to formulate the generalization.

b. Paragraph 5, last sentence—This is cause-and-effect reasoning since it points out the motive for white planter protest. Historian B does try to eliminate the other possible cause by arguing that Democrats were also corrupt when they retook control of the state governments. Most whites, however, may have been genuinely upset with Republican corruption while a few took advantage of the new situation.

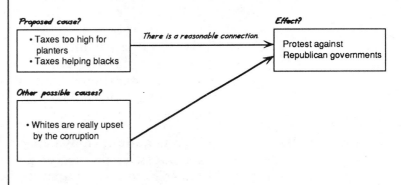

11. Words which make value judgements—Very good and important convey a positive judgement about Republican governments.

12. A, B, and E. Have students explain their answers.

Lesson 7: To What Extent Was Reconstruction a Tragic Era?

Objectives

To identify the main idea
To evaluate evidence
To evaluate cause and effect
To evaluate comparisons
To evaluate generalizations
To evaluate debating reasoning
To identify unstated assumptions

Teaching Ideas

OVERVIEW

This is an interesting lesson which contains two opposing viewpoints (the Dunning School and the Revisionist School) followed by a third viewpoint which takes a somewhat different perspective. It will give you an opportunity to introduce the concept of revisionism. Most students do not realize that traditional interpretations are often revised as historians unearth new information and look at existing information in new ways. Since the interpretations are presented chronologically, you can focus student attention on what effects the time period in which they were written had on the interpretations of history. This issue is dealt with in question 16 on the worksheet (p. 52). Since Historian C's interpretation focuses on the goals and interactions of various groups, especially of freedmen, you can also raise questions about the basic assumptions or world views of the three historians. This issue is dealt with in question 17.

ALTERNATIVE USES

This is quite a challenging lesson since it deals with a complicated topic in a complex way (although a number of issues were deleted from the lesson as noted in the Introduction). If the lesson looks too long or too involved, you might want to have your students undertake Lesson 6 instead. You can simplify this lesson by having students focus on only one or a few issues or answer only selected questions from the worksheet.

APPROACHES TO THE LESSON

Have the class read the Introduction and ask if there are any questions. At this point you could have students do one of the following.

  • Read Historian A, evaluate it, and discuss the interpretation as a class. Read Historian B and then Historian C and repeat the process each time.

- Read all three interpretations, evaluate them according to the ARMEAR model (p. 18) and discuss their evaluations in small groups. Each group could then make a presentation of its evaluations, highlighting two or three key points. Or the class could discuss the three interpretations in general.

- Read all three interpretations, fill in the worksheets (pp. 46–52), discuss their answers in small groups, and discuss the worksheets as a class.

One aspect you might want to focus on is the attitude of each historian toward freedmen. This issue is addressed in questions 2c, 7c, 12c, and 16. Historian A holds racist assumptions, while only Historian C demonstrates a significant role for blacks in Reconstruction.

ADAPTING THE LESSON

Students who need more structure should get the question worksheet. The easier questions are on the main point and evidence. The assumptions questions (number 17) should spark some interesting discussion.

If you have students evaluate the interpretations according to the ARMEAR model, you can give them more structure by having them use Worksheet L ("Analyzing Historical Interpretations"). Again, you might want students to fill in only selected parts of it.

Suggested Answers
HISTORIAN A

1. Main point of Historian A—Reconstruction was a tragic era because of the interference of the Radical Republicans in the life of the South.

2. View of:

a. Radical Republicans
Spiteful toward the South ("vindictive")—Paragraph 5; out for their own power—Paragraph 5; used propaganda—Paragraph 8.

b. Former Confederates and plantation owners
Shocked by Negroes jostling them—Paragraph 4; superior to blacks morally and intellectually—Paragraph 6; decent men—Paragraph 15. Generally, they are portrayed as intelligent people trying to promote order and growth in a difficult situation.

c. Freedmen
Inferior to whites ("well-established traits and habits of Negroes")—Paragraph 6; irresponsible and lazy—Paragraph 7; ignorant, easily manipulated, and corrupt—Paragraph 12. Historian A is racially preju-

diced. Blacks are corrupt but they are not smart enough to be real actors in Reconstruction. They are manipulated by corrupt whites—they have no important role.

d. Carpetbaggers
Corrupt politicians out for power and money—Paragraph 11 and 13; dishonest—Paragraph 12

e. Scalawags
Corrupt politicians out for power and money—Paragraph 11, 13; dishonest—Paragraph 12

3. Group responsible for the failure of Reconstruction: Radical Republicans were mainly responsible (possibly carpetbaggers and scalawags).

4. Evidence

a. Endnote 6—Samuel Hale seems to be a primary source but he could have heard about the blacks voting from someone else. As a Unionist he would probably be sympathetic to the Republicans and to blacks. But as Historian C points out, many Unionists, even in the Republican party, were prejudiced against blacks. So he might have a reason to lie. There is no other evidence corroborating Hale's story.

b. Endnote 8—Primary source, no obvious reason to lie, no corroborating evidence

c. Endnote 10—Primary source, no reason to lie, no corroborating evidence

5. Reasoning

a. Paragraph 14—Cause and effect, comparison (printing in 1869 to all costs in 1860), and generalization. (How large was the sample of states and debts?) In the cause and effect:

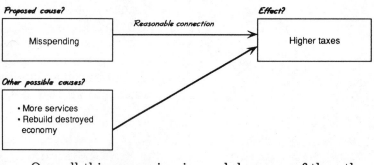

Overall this reasoning is weak because of the other possible causes.

b. Paragraph 15—Cause and effect

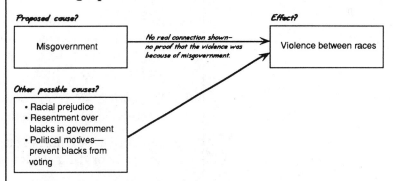

Proposed cause? — Misgovernment

No real connection shown— no proof that the violence was because of misgovernment.

Effect? — Violence between races

Other possible causes?
- Racial prejudice
- Resentment over blacks in government
- Political motives— prevent blacks from voting

Overall, this is weak. The connection is shaky and other causes are more likely. The other cause and effect is that the Union League caused the Ku Klux Klan.

c. Paragraph 17, sentence 3—Generalization (state governments do not represent the Radicals) and comparison—Northern states are compared with Southern states.

HISTORIAN B

6. Main point of Historian B—Reconstruction was not a tragic era—its successes were due to the efforts of the Radical Republicans.

7. View of:

a. Radical Republicans
Good people sincerely trying to help blacks—Paragraph 5.

b. Former Confederates and plantation owners
Racist people who oppressed freedmen through laws (Black Codes) and violence—Paragraph 3.

c. Freedmen
Positive effect on Reconstruction but not a very active role in making decisions during Reconstruction.

d. Carpetbaggers
Some disreputable, but most wanted to help blacks; they were teachers and clergy—Paragraph 7.

e. Scalawags
Four different groups—Historian B does not take a position on them.

8. Historian B primarily blames Southern whites for the failure of Reconstruction.

9. Evidence

a. Endnote 1—Primary source; Humphreys probably believes what he says, but he is also probably trying to get white votes; it is partially supported by the statement by Schurz.

b. Endnote 2—Primary source, no obvious reason to lie, no corroborating evidence

c. Endnote 4—Primary source, no obvious reason to lie, no corroborating evidence

10. Reasoning

a. Paragraph 2—Debating (see page 13 in the "Guide to Critical Thinking"). The key question is: Does this author attack the other views in a fair way? Historian B never uses any unfair arguments, such as *Ad Hominem* or Straw Man (p. 14) in his case against Historian A, and he shows some weaknesses in Historian A's arguments.

b. Paragraph 3, 8th sentence ("Blacks were little better...")—Generalization (maybe some blacks, such as free blacks, escaped the control of the Black Codes) and cause and effect.

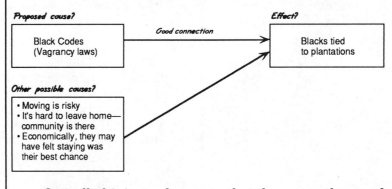

Overall, this is surely a cause, but there are other good causes too.

c. Paragraph 4, last sentence—Cause and effect.

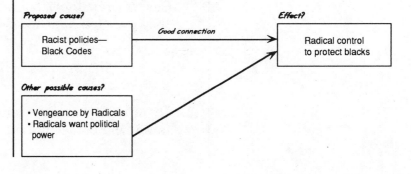

Overall Historian B makes an important point that racist policies came first, so the blame for control rests with Southern whites, not the Radicals. Further, Historian B argues against the other possible causes by saying that the Radicals, as abolitionists, had for years been interested in defending blacks' rights so their motive was not primarily vengeance or political power.

d. Paragraph 12, sentence 1—Comparison. The comparison looks strong. In both cases they are Southern governments. The difference is that they are in different time periods, but the examples of corruption in the second time period may have been selected from a much smaller number of cases of corruption. Thus, the corruption may have been much worse in the Reconstruction governments, but it looks about the same because of the equality of the number of examples.

HISTORIAN C

11. Main point of Historian C—Reconstruction was a failure due to the self-interest and competing beliefs of many groups, violence by southern whites, racism by many groups of whites, and corruption in the Republican governments.

12. View of:

a. Radical Republicans
Sincere people trying to help blacks—Paragraph 10; politicians sensitive to public opinion (and capitalists' opinion especially) and to getting elected—Paragraph 18.

b. Former Confederates and plantation owners
People interested in keeping control of their land and making it productive again, and in taking political control of the South—Paragraphs 6 and 17.

c. Freedmen
Independent-minded people who had very definite ideas about their own best interests. They wanted to control their own lives politically, socially, and economically—Paragraphs 4, 5, and 21.

d. Carpetbaggers
Mostly Civil War veterans, teachers, agents and investors, people who wanted to help blacks and also wanted to get ahead in the South—Paragraph 12.

e. Scalawags
Mostly up-country white farmers who hated planters, wanted lower taxes and more government services for themselves—Paragraph 13; they were somewhat committed to rights for blacks but they were still white with racist attitudes toward blacks.

13. Group responsible for the failure of Reconstruction: Historian C emphasizes the self-interest of all groups as the central cause of the failure of Reconstruction. If any group gets more blame, it is non-Republican Southern whites because of their oppression of blacks, especially their violence.

14. Evidence

a. Endnote 3—Primary source, no reason to lie, no supporting evidence

b. Endnote 7, House Report—Primary source, reason to lie, the other part of the endnote supplies supporting evidence

c. Endnote 16—Secondary source, no reason to lie, no supporting evidence

15. Reasoning

a. Paragraph 2—Generalization about the North prospering, but Historian C breaks down the generalization into subgroups of the whole North (see pp. 8–11 on making generalizations) which strengthens the generalization.

b. Paragraph 5, sentence 2—Comparison. The cases have differences, but the fact that freedmen in many societies have wanted land ownership shows that it was an important need to them.

c. Paragraph 10, sentence 2—Generalization. This is weak since only one case, Thaddeus Stevens, is mentioned to represent the whole group of Radical Republicans. If many or most of the Radicals had not been abolitionists then this point is erroneous.

d. Paragraph 20—Cause and effect. Many causes for the failures of Reconstruction are outlined, and the connections between the causes and effect are well explained in the main part of the argument.

GENERAL QUESTIONS

16. Dates

    Historian A (1907, 1937)—In these earlier time periods racism was more obvious and the racism in this interpretation is blatant.

    Historian B (1965)—With the Civil Rights Movement in full swing historians looked more closely at what had been happening to blacks since slavery. If whites were mistreating blacks in the 1950s and 1960s then maybe they were the cause of problems in the 1860s and 1870s.

    Historian C (1988)—By the 1980s historians had seen the central role that blacks played in the Civil Rights Movement. Blacks were no longer viewed as pawns in a larger game, but rather as players who made decisions and influenced other groups. They also had seen two decades of social-history research—the study of ordinary people in their everyday lives. This study of how ordinary groups influence politics and life is evident in Historian C's interpretation.

17. Assumptions (There is a lot of room here for disagreement. Simply let each person give a reason for his or her choice.)

    a. B,C

    b. C

    c. A

    d. C

    e. B,C

    f. B,C

    g. A

    h. A

    i. C

    j. C

Lesson 8: What Does Visual Evidence Show about Reconstruction Attitudes toward Blacks?

Objectives

To find the main idea
To evaluate visual evidence

Teaching Ideas

Students will be able to evaluate the drawings in much more depth if they have already studied Reconstruction in some detail.

Have students read the directions, examine the drawings, and write their answers to the question. Then discuss their answers in small groups and as a class.

The question involves a number of steps to answer, so you might want to break it down into subquestions such as the following.

Drawing 1

1. How are blacks shown? (Sympathetically or unsympathetically?)

2. Why is the woman asking "And Not This Man?"

3. What's the point?

Drawing 2

4. How are blacks shown?

5. What's the point?

Drawing 3

6. How are blacks shown?

7. What's the point?

Overall

8. How did opinion about blacks change from 1865 to 1874?

9. Based on your knowledge of Reconstruction why did opinion about blacks change this way?

Thus, there are two basic questions involved: How did opinion of blacks change and why did it change?

Another interesting question is the extent to which the

press represents public opinion in general. Did *Harper's Weekly* represent the views of the Republican Party or of the general public?

Suggested Answers

Questions in the lesson (not the nine questions above)

1. The first drawing shows the black soldier as an upstanding citizen who had earned the right to vote (implied by the question "And Not This Man?"). The second drawing shows the freedman as innocent victim of Irish immigrants, Confederate veterans, and Wall Street investors. These three groups were thought to be the basic parts of the Democratic Party at that time. The third drawing shows black legislators as buffoons making a mockery of democratic government.

2. The reasons for the views of blacks may be as follows. The first drawing was done soon after the end of the Civil War when the Emancipation Proclamation and black heroics in fighting for the North were recent. The second drawing was done after the Johnson governments had been in control in the South. Public opinion in the North was unfavorable toward these Democratic state governments. The third drawing was done after the Republican governments had been in power for several years and after charges of corruption and fraud had been made repeatedly. Note the racist characteristics of the black characters in this drawing and of the Irishman in the second drawing.

Lesson 9: Why Was the Fourteenth Amendment Passed?

Objectives

To analyze a primary source
To use relevant information to make and test hypotheses

Teaching Ideas

OVERVIEW

The Fourteenth Amendment is commonly thought to be one of the most important parts of the Constitution. This lesson focuses primarily on why the amendment was passed but it also asks students to consider some of the effects of the amendment. The effects of the amendment are quite difficult to figure out as they are based on the language in the amendment such as "due process of law" and "equal protection of the laws." Justices have struggled for decades trying to define those phrases.

THE LESSON

Have students read over the amendment and ask volunteers to explain in their own words what each section means. Tell the class that sections 1 and 2 are the most important parts of the amendment and most questions will be about them. Students should then answer the three questions below the amendment (p. 58). Tell them that they are just hypothesizing—guessing is encouraged. Do not discuss student answers. Have them go on to the next section, read the sequence of proposals and the relevant information, then answer the questions (p. 62–63). Have students in groups of three discuss their answers and then discuss them as a class.

STUDENT PREPARATION

Although the introduction gives an overview of Reconstruction, it would be better if students had already done Lesson 6 or 7 on Reconstruction or read about Reconstruction in their textbook. The more historical context students know, the better they will understand the passage of the Fourteenth Amendment.

EXTENDING THE LESSON

Have students write an essay on one of the following: "A History of the Passage of the Fourteenth Amendment," or "The Meaning of the Fourteenth Amendment."

ALTERING THE LESSON

You can shorten the lesson by having students answer only selected questions. Question 9 is important to select because of the relationship of women's rights to blacks' rights.

Suggested Answers

1. Congress wanted to make sure blacks' rights would be protected no matter who was in control of the govern-

ment in Washington. That's one motive among many that historians have suggested.

2. Congress was not ready to impose black suffrage on the country. Many people in the North were opposed to blacks voting. By giving the South an option on black suffrage, some members of Congress felt the Amendment had a realistic chance for passage and ratification.

3. Two groups that would have been upset were Southern whites and feminists. Note the word "male" in section 2 as a qualification for voting. A third group was abolitionists and Radicals who wanted black suffrage.

4. Relevant Information M suggests that voters in the North were not ready for black suffrage, and 1866 was an election year for Congress (J). Members of Congress were ambivalent about extending the powers of the national government too far (I).

5. Relevant Information A shows that blacks had not been considered citizens in the Constitution. Relevant Information B and C shows that hostility to the idea of civil rights existed and that someday a popular majority could overturn civil rights legislation with new legislation. A Constitutional Amendment would prevent these changes and support equality before the law (K). Relevant Information P and Q suggest that there was a need to extend the national Bill of Rights to all citizens, overriding state constitutions.

6. Relevant Information D indicates that Proposal II was introduced to prevent the South from counting the freedmen to gain representatives and take over Congress while denying them the right to vote.

7. Relevant Information E and F show that Northern states, especially New England would not like Proposal II because either their representation in Congress would be reduced or they would have to give the vote to women and foreigners. (Heaven forbid!)

8. Relevant Information G suggests the possibility that the Southern states would use non-racial methods such as literacy tests and property qualifications to keep poor blacks and whites from voting while still counting them for representation in Congress.

9. The word "male" in Proposal IV would prevent non-racial discrimination by using literacy tests or prop-

erty qualifications to regulate voters as described in the answer to question 8. According to Relevant Information H, R, S, T, and U women's rights activists would have been very upset by the word "male" inserted into the amendment. Women had worked for two decades to destroy the centuries-old assumption that political rights, including suffrage, applied only to men. The insertion of the word "male" made sexual discrimination explicit in the Constitution for the first time, setting the women's rights movement back. Women had set aside their demand for suffrage in order to support the abolitionists (H). Further, they had supported Phillips in the American Anti-Slavery Society (R). But Phillips said women's suffrage would have to wait (S), and so did Congress. Women activists were upset. The word "male" was inserted despite the opposition because Republicans felt they could not realistically get rights for both blacks and women at the same time. There was too much opposition.

10. The Memphis riot may have helped get the bill passed by Congress. The New Orleans riot may have helped get it ratified. Both riots showed the failure of President Johnson's policies in the South.

11. There is not really enough information here to answer this question, but it may be helpful for students to speculate on the effects that the Fourteenth Amendment had. Relevant Information L shows it may have been framed in general terms on purpose, to be left to courts to interpret. Section 2 of the amendment was temporary until the Fifteenth Amendment was ratified. Section 1, with the phrases "due process of law" and "equal protection of the laws," had tremendous impact on the country by allowing citizens to sue for violations of their rights according to the Bill of Rights in the federal Constitution. The revolutionary potential of the amendment lay dormant (see, for example, the *Slaughterhouse Cases* of 1873) until the 1950s when blacks used it effectively in the Civil Rights Movement. Active liberal courts, especially the Warren Court, applied the Fourteenth Amendment to a wide range of cases involving individual rights.

UNIT 3
INDUSTRIALIZATION AND RESPONSE

Lesson 10: Evaluating Evidence

Objective

To evaluate evidence

Teaching Ideas

This is meant to be a short reinforcement lesson. Part A breaks the skill down into subquestions. So with students who are having difficulty with the skill just do Part A.

Remind students that strength means more reliable and weakness means less reliable. We are not focusing as much on what the speakers say or the strength of their convictions, but on whether we can believe what they say.

Have students fill in the sheet and go over it as a class.

Suggested Answers

1. [Bill and Terry]

    a. Yes, he has a reason to lie.

    b. Primary

    c. No, there is no supporting evidence.

    d. Very unreliable

    e. Ask Terry about the jewelry, and search both Bill and Terry.

2. [John D. Rockefeller and Ida Tarbell]

    a. Yes, he has a reason to lie.

    b. Rockefeller has more reason, but Tarbell has a reason to exaggerate the story to gain notoriety as an investigative journalist.

    c. Yes, he is a primary source.

    d. She was around at the time, but she probably did not actually witness his actions. So, she is a secondary source.

    e. No supporting evidence

    f. Each is weak in a different way. Rockefeller has great incentive to protect himself. Tarbell is a secondary source and may be exaggerating. Let students explain their reasons.

    g. Look up records of Rockefeller's dealings, and research what businessmen said about his practices.

3. [Gwen]

STRENGTHS
- primary source
- reason to lie

WEAKNESSES
- no other supporting evidence

The coach can verify the claim by making Gwen do some drills or having her run. That strengthens the claim somewhat—people are more likely to tell the truth when they know their story could be checked for verification.

4. [Andrew Carnegie]

STRENGTHS
- primary source

WEAKNESSES
- reason to lie
- no supporting evidence.

5. [Gustavus Myers]

STRENGTHS
- no obvious reason to lie

WEAKNESSES
- secondary source (you can tell by the dates)
- no supporting evidence.

6. [John Moody]

STRENGTHS
- no obvious reason to lie
- has supporting evidence

WEAKNESSES
- it is hard to tell if Moody is a primary or secondary source

Moody probably did not witness the formation of US Steel but he did not need to in order to make the claim that it was the largest corporation. He probably did not get all the records himself and make the calculations so he is probably a secondary source.

7. [Henry Ford]

STRENGTHS
- primary source
- maybe no reason to lie

WEAKNESSES
- no supporting evidence
- he might have a reason to lie

Since the "Model T" was successful Ford might be trying to claim credit for the idea of concentrating only on it.

Lesson 11: Identifying and Evaluating Comparisons

Objectives

To recognize comparison reasoning
To evaluate comparison arguments

Teaching Ideas

The first section of the worksheet can be done quickly. Have students write in their answers, share them in small groups, and discuss them as a class.

The second part is more difficult. Have students do problem 9 and discuss it as a class. Then have them try problem 10, share their answers in small groups, and discuss them as a class.

Suggested Answers

1. N
2. N
3. C
4. C Compares GNP in two different time periods
5. N
6. N
7. N
8. C Note the difference between question 5 and this argument. The two key words are "increased" (compares production over time) and "faster" (compares prices to production).

9. There may have been more tests in the European History course and the questions may have been picky and difficult. The teacher in the U.S. History course may grade the essays generously, while the European History teacher may never give an "A." If this student defines "harder" only in terms of amount of work, and if the European History teacher did not give a research paper or some other assignment not included in this student's definition of homework, then this is a reasonable argument.

10. An obvious difference is the larger economy and greater economic growth of the United States. This is an important difference.

Lesson 12: Identifying and Evaluating Cause-and-Effect Reasoning

Objectives

To identify cause-and-effect reasoning
To assess the strength of cause-and-effect relationships
To encourage students to think of alternative causes

Teaching Ideas

This is a reinforcement lesson on cause-and-effect reasoning.

Have students do the first problem in each section (questions 1 and 7), then discuss their answers before they proceed with the other problems in the section.

Suggested Answers

1. C   Cause—excellent relief pitching; effect—first place.
2. C   Cause—AAA maps; effect—fastest route.
3. N
4. N
5. C   Cause—industrialization; effect—greater distance between rich and poor.
6. N
7. This argument considers many causes for industrialization in the United States. It is difficult to think of other causes. Some of the causes have a logical connection to the effect. But some do not and no explanation of the connections is given.

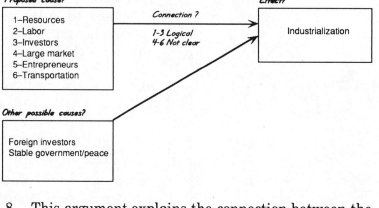

8. This argument explains the connection between the cause and the effect but does not consider other causes for the increased bankruptcies among the railroads. Another interesting point in this argument is the

correlation between bankruptcies and the depression: increased bankruptcies among railroads when the economy got worse (depression), therefore the depression caused the increase in bankruptcies. This is not, however, the correlation as cause fallacy (p. 6) because the author explains how depression caused bankruptcies.

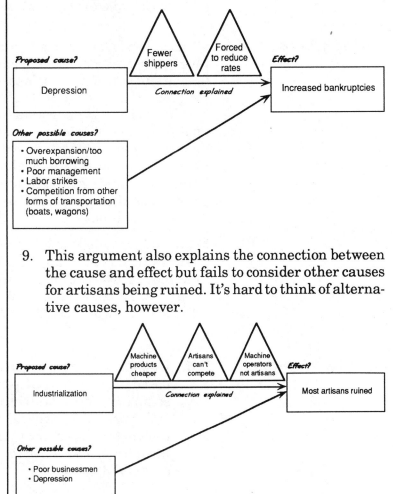

9. This argument also explains the connection between the cause and effect but fails to consider other causes for artisans being ruined. It's hard to think of alternative causes, however.

Lesson 13: Identifying and Analyzing Types of Reasoning

Objectives

To identify and evaluate comparisons
To identify and evaluate generalizations
To identify and evaluate cause and effect

Teaching Ideas

This lesson is meant to give students practice in identifying types of reasoning and then evaluating that reasoning. Some students may be able to evaluate reasoning when it is given to them on a worksheet, yet they will struggle in evaluating it in an interpretation because they cannot pick out the types of reasoning used in various parts of the interpretation. This lesson helps students with the transition from the skill of evaluating reasoning when the types of reasoning are given to them, to the combination of skills used in both picking out and evaluating reasoning in interpretations.

Have students do Problem 1 and discuss it as a class. Ask if students have any questions about how to fill in the sheet. Have students fill in the rest of the sheet, discuss their answers in small groups, and discuss the group answers as a class.

Suggested Answers

1. Uniforms—This is a generalization that seems to be based on a statistical survey of men's sizes. If the sample is representative, the standard size uniforms will work. This type of thinking became popular around the time of the Civil War, according to Daniel Boorstin in *The Americans: The Democratic Experience* (1973).

2. Andrew Carnegie—This is a generalization. We should ask: "Are these two benefits representative of all the things he did?" Even if we could show bad effects of Carnegie (such as low wages or pollution) that would not show the argument to be wrong. The argument focuses only on benefits. Since his philanthropy probably had many diverse effects itself, the argument seems reasonable. We might want to ask if the money he used for philanthropy would have been better used by his workers or other common people, but again, that does not hit the point of the argument. (It says he benefited mankind, not that he benefited mankind as much as others might have.)

3. Trusts—This is primarily a cause-and-effect argument (it is also a generalization). By asking "Is there a reasonable connection?" we see that the author does not show how trusts caused the evils of industrial America. Some historians, such as Historian B in Lesson 16, argue that trusts helped the country on balance. By asking "Are there other possible causes for this effect?" we see that many factors (government corruption; increased, unplanned urban growth; increased cotton production in India; alcoholism; inflation; deflation; etc.) were responsible for evils in America in the late 1800s. This argument is very weak.

4. Loans to Railroads—This is primarily cause and effect. The connection makes sense although it is not explained. The railroads would have reason to rush construction, in spite of quality, in order to get their money faster. Other possible causes for rapid construction are to keep labor and overhead costs down. Still, if the government had said it would not pay until it inspected the quality of the construction, the railroads would probably have been more careful. Or, if the government paid by the hour, the railroads still would not be done!

5. Watered stock—This is primarily a generalization. We do not know what type of sample was done so we do not know if it is representative of the captains of industry in general.

6. GNP per person—This is both a generalization and a comparison. The comparison can be evaluated by asking about similarities and differences. The similarity of using per capita GNP makes this argument much stronger than if it did not use it. The GNP could have risen but the population could have increased more making Americans worse off financially. If inflation went up more than GNP in this time period, however, Americans might still have been worse off financially. Inflation is an important possible difference between the two time periods. As any economist will tell you, real GNP per capita is much more accurate for comparative statistics.

Lesson 14: Should the Government Role Be Laissez-faire or the General Welfare State?

Objectives

To support arguments with evidence
To evaluate cause and effect
To evaluate comparison reasoning
To evaluate generalizations
To identify unstated assumptions
To evaluate the reasoning that students use themselves
To formulate arguments to defend a particular point of view

Teaching Ideas

OVERVIEW

This lesson focuses on the competing philosophies of political economy in the late 1800s. As explained in the introduction to the lesson, thinkers in the United States and Europe struggled with the issue of the proper role of government in a rapidly industrializing and urbanizing society. The ten thinkers presented here will give students the opportunity to examine the issue for themselves.

The summaries of each of the thinkers are cursory and incomplete. Ideas from a number of writings were melded into a single argument which is an injustice to the author's original statements. In some cases, ideas of other thinkers who agreed with the ten summarized were added. For example, Richard T. Ely was the leader of the new school of political economy which was comprised of many other economists. Some of the ideas in the summary of Ely's argument came from these other economists.

INTRODUCING THE LESSON

Begin the lesson by having students fill in the worksheet "Laissez-faire Survey" (p. 90) and discuss their responses. Then have students read the introduction to the lesson. Ask what the following mean: laissez-faire, Darwinism, social Darwinism, the Social Gospel, and the general welfare state. You might also want to ask what factors in American History would have made Americans in 1865 favor laissez-faire and what factors would have made them favor the general welfare state. This question forces students to draw upon their pool of historical knowledge.

Factors favoring laissez-faire are

(1)   America's struggle against Britain made us anti-big government;

(2) belief in natural law (like survival of the fittest);

(3) faith in the individual—frontier experience, transcendentalism, Christianity;

(4) natural rights—wary of government oppression;

(5) Jefferson's minimum government beliefs;

(6) Jackson's anti-bank crusade and veto message.

Factors favoring the general welfare state are

(1) Hamilton's program—National Bank, etc.;

(2) Clay's American System;

(3) the protective tariff;

(4) the expansion of government during the Civil War.

TEACHING THE LESSON

At this point, there are two possible ways to proceed. The recommended format is a debate on the issue:

To what extent should government interfere in society?

Clarify the laissez-faire and general welfare state positions on the question. Tell students to read the ten thinkers and fill in the worksheet "Arguments for and against Laissez-faire" (p. 89) and the focus question (p. 88) in preparation for a debate on the above issue. Ask for a show of hands as to who supports the laissez-faire position, who opposes it, and who is undecided. Use the undecideds to balance off the pro and con groups. Tell the class to divide into groups of four. Each student is assigned a thinker (or two) and told to present the thinker's best arguments to the group. Divide the ten thinkers in this way:

Pro Laissez-Faire		Pro Welfare State	
Student 1	Smith (A)	Student 5	George/Veblen (F/J)
Student 2	Spencer (B)	Student 6	Ely (G)
Student 3	Sumner (C)	Student 7	Gladden (H)
Student 4	Carnegie/Alger (D/E)	Student 8	Ward (I)

One student in each group records the best arguments. The students then debate 4 against 4, or the whole class debates the issue. In the large group debate, you could write down a few of the arguments made and duplicate them for students to analyze for the next class. (An example of a worksheet on a debate is on pp. 89–90 of the *Teacher's Guide*.) The analysis of their own arguments will help students recognize their own use of reasoning, evidence, and so forth.

You could also make a list of some issues raised in the debate about the role of government in society, and tell students to research one of those issues. Each student must find one piece of information from U.S. history, 1865 to 1924, to support his or her side in the debate. Encourage students to question and evaluate the sources of information their opponents give.

(Possible issues raised: Do the rich deserve their wealth? Should there be inheritance tax? Are there hard-working poor people? Is government always inefficient and corrupt? Is there really fair competition? What should be done about monopolies? Do the rich manipulate the market? Should self-interest be the driving force in society? Should we have more growth, more freedom, or more equality?)

ALTERING THE LESSON

The second way to proceed with the lesson is to have students fill in the worksheet questions on the Ten Thinkers. (p. 83–87) This alternative to a debate allows you to focus on specific points of each thinker, and the lesson will be completed more quickly.

You could shorten the lesson even further by having students read only one or two thinkers from each side of the government issue.

TROUBLESHOOTING

Large group debates may become dominated by a few of the more vocal students in class. One method we have used is to put students who have been monopolizing the debate into the "penalty box" for a few minutes—they cannot speak. It is worth noting that many of the students who do not speak in debates are listening and learning. If you want more involvement, focus more on small group debates.

Group work can degenerate into socializing. Allow only a short time (3 minutes?) to prepare for the debate.

EVALUATION

You can evaluate the lesson by having students write an essay in favor of or against laissez-faire in which they are to label their thesis with a "T" in the margin, three arguments with "A" in the margin, and three pieces of evidence with "E" in the margin.

Alternatively, you could test students on the arguments of each thinker. If you want to do that, feel free to make up a test.

Suggested Answers

THINKER A—ADAM SMITH

1. The sum of self-interest in individual transactions is the total of the self-interest of all members of society or the general welfare. The market's "invisible hand" converts self-interest to the benefit of the whole society.

2. Society is too complex for rational thought by any person or group, which is what government is. Government can never react fast enough to all those transactions in the marketplace, so it is by nature inefficient, whereas the market *is* the transactions—it reacts immediately and constantly.

3. This is the composition fallacy. A transaction may be best for both parties, but may hurt society, [such as drugs for guns]. Another problem is that a person may feel he is getting the best deal when he is not. Or the circumstances may be such that the best deal someone can get may not be very good. A monopoly may be selling water or oil for exorbitant prices and people may buy it as the best deal they can get under the circumstances. But such a situation hardly brings about benefit to the general welfare.

THINKER B—HERBERT SPENCER

4. This is a comparison. The two cases are similar in some ways (humans are part of the animal kingdom), but they are different in that humans have the ability to affect nature, and society is different from nature in many ways.

5. He assumes that the rich have merit and the poor are good for nothing—lazy.

6. Government programs limit peoples' freedom, interfere with survival of the fittest, and have negative unintended consequences. Government cannot make any significant difference in the slow evolution of society (the gigantic plan)—it only perverts it.

THINKER C—WILLIAM GRAHAM SUMNER

7. The rich advance society and the poor are lazy.

8. Government help diverts resources to the unproductive part of the economy, which leads to less economic growth. This leads to fewer goods and services for each person. Everyone is now worse off!

9. The forgotten man (middle-class citizen) is hurt by government interference.

THINKER D—ANDREW CARNEGIE

10. This is a generalization. It depends on how well the market works to translate self-interest into benefit for the general welfare. (See the answer to question 3.)

THINKER E—HORATIO ALGER	11.	Poor people deserve to be poor. If they would work hard, they would get ahead.
THINKER F—HENRY GEORGE	12.	Rich people get their money from increasing land values, which they did nothing to improve and therefore from which they do not deserve the value.
THINKER G—RICHARD T. ELY	13.	Three weaknesses are: (1) Laissez-faire is too simple for complex industrial society; (2) man is not motivated by self-interest alone; (3) self-interest does not necessarily bring about benefit to society.

14. The weaknesses are:

a. Government—government is corrupt because belief in laissez-faire weakens it so much; with so little regulation, everyone's liberty is reduced.

b. Workers' wages—workers do not have an even chance negotiating individually with owners. They should have the right to unionize.

c. Individualism—extreme individualism is unchristian.

THINKER H—WASHINGTON GLADDEN	15.	Workers are much more than a product, they are children of God.

16. The corporations get progressively more immoral, since the most immoral among the businesses have advantages by being immoral.

THINKER I—LESTER FRANK WARD	17.	Humans are different from animals precisely because they are intelligent and can and do interfere with nature.

18. The government is inefficient because it does not use scientific principles to make decisions. It is dominated by the rich at this point because of the weakness brought about by the belief in laissez-faire.

19. It is cause and effect. He sees government corruption and perversion by the rich as an effect of a weak government. But it might be that government will always be corrupted no matter what its size. In fact, a large government may be corrupted more by the rich and powerful.

THINKER J—THORSTEIN VEBLEN	20.	The rich businessmen make their money by manipulating investments and living off the industrious people. This actually hurts society by limiting improvements rather than expanding them.

21. Veblen stereotypes (p. 10) rich businessmen and investors. Not all of them are speculators.

EXAMPLE OF DEBATE TRAN-
SCRIPTION AND QUESTIONS

This is a transcription from a debate in an average 11th grade U.S. History class. It is included here as an example of a way to get students to look at the arguments they themselves use in a debate. Jot down arguments during the debate, then write them up as shown here. Give students the transcript along with analysis questions such as the ones on the next page.

This transcript is meant only as an example. You will want to make a transcript of the arguments your students use in their debate.

I. Laissez-faire (hereafter LF)—Self-interest motivates people. Self-interest differs from person to person. When government interferes it is for the general good, not for individual good. So, government interference hurts some motivated people but doesn't necessarily help motivated people.

II. Welfare State (hereafter WS)—But the rich already own almost everything, so poor people who are motivated still can't get ahead. Government interference is necessary.

III. LF—If the poor work hard they can get ahead. After all, most rich people started poor. Look at Andrew Carnegie.

IV. WS—Most rich people did not start poor. People have to be lucky to be rich. It's wrong to base our society on luck. We need government interference to promote more equality.

V. LF—Government meddling in the economy slows down economic growth, since the market is more efficient than government.

VI. WS—Without government restrictions, a few rich would control a lot of the economy.

VII. LF—That's not true. Actually, rich investments help everyone by improving the economy. Investing in an industry improves the production which leads to a better economy.

VIII. WS—But the rich get all the profits.

IX. LF—The rich deserve the profits since they create things which society wants.

X. WS—We have to choose whether we want a larger, unequal society or a smaller economy with a more equal society.

XI. LF—What are you, a communist?

XII. WS—No. The poor don't have the same opportunity to make money once some people are rich. They need and deserve help.

XIII. LF—The poor are behind because it's like the jungle—it's survival of the fittest.

XIV. WS—But helping the poor means higher taxes. Why should the successful person get penalized and have to pay higher taxes for his success?

Questions

A. What is the conclusion of:
    1. Sentence I:
    2. Sentence VI:
    3. Sentence XV:

B. What is a word which makes a value judgement in:
    4. Sentence V:
    5. Sentence IX:

C. What word needs to be defined better in:
    6. Sentence II:
    7. Sentence XV:

D. What is a value expressed in:
    8. Sentence II:

E. What is the assumption in:
    9. Sentence XIV:

F. Evaluate the reasoning used in:
    10. Sentence III:
    11. Sentence VII:
    12. Sentence XIII:
    13. Sentence V:
    14. Sentence X:

G. What is a fallacy in:
    15. Sentence XI:

Lesson 15: What Is Significant about the Life of John D. Rockefeller

Objectives

To recognize unstated assumptions and values
To recognize that frame of reference influences selection of information

Teaching Ideas

Start the lesson by having students read the introduction to the Biography Worksheet (p. 94) and then brainstorm to generate questions to ask in their interviews of each other. You might want to list suggestions for questions on the board. If students can't think of many questions to ask, use the Suggested Questions below to help them generate more questions. After the interview and the oral reports on each other, students will have a better idea of how to write the biography of Rockefeller.

Have students write a maximum 300-word biography of Rockefeller as instructed on page 91 of the student book. Remind them to focus on what kind of person Rockefeller was. What is significant about him? What can we learn from him? If possible, they should consider what Rockefeller shows about American society at that time, but that may be too much to fit into such a short assignment.

Obviously there is too much information provided to fit into a 300-word essay. This will force students to select information based on their notions of "significance," and from these selections the class can identify unstated assumptions or values.

When students have written their biographies of Rockefeller, instruct them to go back to the information in the student text and note in their essays the number of each piece of information they used.

Next, have students pair up and discuss which information they selected. Why was the information similar or different? What made certain information significant?

Then discuss the question of significance as a class.

Allow students to rewrite their biographies in light of the discussion and resubmit them the next day.

Lesson 16, on the Standard Oil Company, is a natural follow up to this lesson.

SUGGESTED QUESTIONS

1. What do you do with your free time?

2. What is your favorite thing (and your least favorite thing) about school/work/sports/etc.?

3. What are you best at? worst at?

4. Do you work? At what? When did you start?

5. What do you think about the groups on campus? Who do you interact with?

6. What extracurricular activities are you involved in?

7. What do you want to accomplish in your life?

8. How would you describe yourself?

9. How would your best friend describe you? your worst enemy? your family?

10. What have you done that you are most proud of?

11. What do you like best about yourself? What do you like least?

12. What do you like best (and least) about other people?

13. What are your responsibilities at home?

14. Do you put things off that you don't like or do the worst tasks first and save the best for last?

15. Describe your personal values.

16. What is your philosophy of life?

17. What are the three most important things in your life right now?

18. Where do you want to be at 30—personally, financially, spiritually, geographically, etc.?

19. What has been your most important experience in life so far?

20. What is your most important goal for the next year? next five years? next ten years?

21. In one sentence, what do you want people to say of you after you're dead?

22. When and where were you born?

23. What early memories do you have that you feel have shaped the way you are now?

24. What was the most important thing that your mother/father ever said to you?

25. What would your mother/father say are your best qualities? your worst qualities?

26. What is your earliest memory of your mother/father?

27. Do you have brothers/sisters? How do you get along with your brother(s)/sister(s)?

28. What are your mother/father like? your brother(s)/sister(s)? your family life?

29. How has your family influenced the way in which you look at yourself? at life?

30. What person outside of your family has influenced you the most?

31. Who do you admire? want to be like? see as a role model?

Suggested Answers

There are no specific answers in this lesson. By asking how students decided what to include in their biographies you can focus on student assumptions about what is important in history. For example, if many students choose information about Rockefeller's childhood you can ask: "Are you saying that childhood experiences are very important to how adults act?" If questions of immoral behavior are chosen frequently, ask why ethical versus unethical behavior is so important.

Lesson 16: Introduction to the Oil Business

Objectives

To identify the main idea
To evaluate evidence
To evaluate cause and effect
To evaluate comparisons
To evaluate generalizations
To identify unstated assumptions and value claims
To relate relevant information to hypotheses

Teaching Ideas

PREPARATION

One way to start the lesson is to ask students what a monopoly is. Technically, in economics, a monopoly has three parts: one seller, a barrier to entry against new businesses, and no substitute for the product being sold. Since a monopoly receives artificially high prices, it would need some way of preventing new businesses, attracted by the high profits, from coming into the industry. Also, consumers would turn to substitutes with prices so high, so there can be no substitutes available. In the real world a product with one seller having complete control of price, a perfect barrier to entry, and no substitute is virtually impossible, so we normally talk about a situation that is close to monopoly as a monopoly.

Discuss the concept and then tell students that in this lesson we will be looking at the Standard Oil Company, run by John D. Rockefeller. Standard Oil attained a monopoly of the United States oil-refining business in the late 1800s. The lesson contains two viewpoints of Standard Oil and Mr. Rockefeller's business practices.

APPROACHES TO THE LESSON

Have the class read the Introduction and ask if there are any questions. At this point you could have students do one of the following:

- read Historian A, evaluate it, and discuss the interpretation as a class. Then read Historian B and repeat the process.

- read both interpretations, evaluate them according to the ARMEAR model (p. 18) and discuss their evaluations in groups of three.

- read both interpretations, fill in the worksheets for them (pp. 103–9), discuss their answers in small groups, and discuss the worksheets as a class.

- choose one of the interpretations and defend it in a debate: "John D. Rockefeller: Robber Baron or Industrial Statesman?"

ADAPTING THE LESSON

Students who need more structure should probably use the question worksheet. The easier questions are on the main idea and evidence, while the more challenging questions are on reasoning and assumptions. You can make the assumption questions much easier, however, by using the worksheet "Assumptions of Historian's A and B." Once students see the statements they are much more likely to identify which historian would agree with them. The sheet is also useful for initiating a discussion of the students' assumptions and values and how those assumptions and values influence their evaluations of the two interpretations. The suggested answers for questions 7 and 17 give answers for the assumptions worksheet.

If you have students evaluate the interpretations according to the ARMEAR model you can give them structure by having them use Worksheet L ("Analyzing Historical Interpretations," p. 52, Teacher's Guide). Again, you might want students to fill in only selected parts of it.

If your students did Lesson 15 they will have a body of relevant information about Rockefeller to assist them in evaluating the two viewpoints in this lesson. Even if they have not read Lesson 15, question 20 on the worksheet for this lesson alerts them to look at it.

The suggested answers are for the questions on the Historians' Viewpoints. No answers are suggested for the worksheet "Questions about Standard Oil/Rockefeller."

Suggested Answers
HISTORIAN A

1. Main point of Historian A—Rockefeller used unethical business practices, so he should not be regarded as a business hero.

2. Evidence in endnote 1—No specific owner is cited for Rockefeller's statements, so there is no specific source. This part of the evidence would be considered hearsay in court. The evidence by Frank is specific, however. We do not know if Frank was present when the deals were made, so we do not know if Frank is a primary source. Frank has no obvious reason to lie, but the owners do. The two parts of the endnote support each other (corroboration). Overall, we would like to see eyewitness documentation of Rockefeller saying this.

3. Evidence in endnote 2—Mr. Alexander is a primary source, but he has a reason to lie, since he may resent Rockefeller after having to sell out. Historian B makes this very point in paragraphs 13 and 14.

4. Evidence in endnote 4—All three pieces of evidence are secondary. Teagle and the Marietta refiner each have a reason to lie. The black boy losing his job is unclear. He may have said he received bribes to cover up something else. On the other hand, the evidence of a bribe may have been very impressive. The three pieces of evidence support each other.

5. Last sentence in paragraph 6—This is cause and effect.

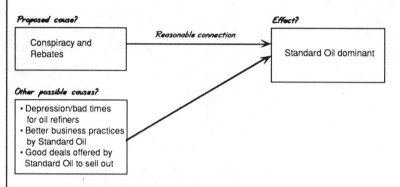

Overall: This reasoning is weak because the other possible causes are as likely as rebates to lead to Standard Oil dominance. Historian A should show why rebates were the key.

6. Third sentence in paragraph 10—This is a generalization. The historian brings up three cases to show that the practice was widespread. We do not know if these were the only cases or if they represent a wider number of occurrences. Three cases shows it happened more than once but doesn't necessarily show company policy. On the other hand, the evidence of forms to write information about competing companies seems to show it was company policy.

7. Unstated assumption—There are many possible assumptions Historian A makes, three of which are on the worksheet "Assumptions of Historians A and B"—Numbers 1, 3, and 4 (a & d).

8. Value—Historian A believes in values such as justice, equal opportunity, and honesty.

HISTORIAN B

9. Main point of Historian B—While John D. Rockefeller made some mistakes and sometimes used ruthless business tactics, he was a great business leader—foremost in business and foremost in philanthropy.

10. Evidence in endnote 2—The railroad commission is a secondary source, although it undoubtedly took evidence from primary sources; Flagler is primary. Both sources have a reason to lie. The two sources corroborate each other. Overall, this is strong evidence—it is quite likely that rebates were common before Standard Oil began business.

11. Evidence in endnote 6—Rockefeller is a primary source, but he has an obvious reason to lie and no one else verifies that he said it this way. This is weak evidence. Students will have to understand *Ibid* to evaluate this evidence.

12. Evidence in endnote 8—Mr. Tucker is a primary source who has no obvious reason to lie, and who is supported by the evidence in endnote 9. This is strong evidence for Tucker's company, but should not be generalized to all or most of the companies which sold out to Standard Oil.

13. Paragraphs 4 and 5—This is cause and effect.

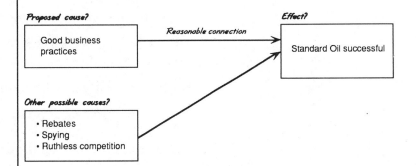

Historian B should show that rebates were not as important as good business practices. As with Historian A, the other causes seem as likely as Historian B's cause.

14. Paragraph 7—This is a comparison. There are some significant differences between the two cases. Consumers are not using discounts to drive other consumers out of business. The end result of discounts for consumers is not a monopoly as in the case of Standard Oil. Also, the general public may agree that at least the discount prices must be posted for all to see (as opposed to secret rebates).

15. Paragraph 13, sentence 2—"Most" indicates a generalization. No evidence is offered to show that most companies were unprofitable, so we do not know how

strong this generalization is. An interesting point is that Rockefeller may have caused these oil refineries to become unprofitable, due, for example, to his rebate advantages. Then he justified buying them out at very low prices because they were now "unprofitable."

16. Paragraph 15, sentence 4—This is also a generalization. One case is offered which is certainly not enough to show that most refiners sold out willingly.

17. Unstated assumption—Historian B would most likely agree with numbers 2, 5, and 6 on the worksheet "Assumptions of Historians A and B."

18. Value—Historian B believes in values such as efficiency, hard work, risk taking, freedom, and economic growth.

GENERAL QUESTIONS

19. Some points on which they agree:

   • Drawbacks were an unfair business practice.

   • Rockefeller was wrong to join the South Improvement Company.

   • Rockefeller was a very good businessman.

   • Rockefeller was a good family man and had other upright qualities outside of his business.

   • Rockefeller accepted rebates.

20. Relevant information (from Lesson 15, pp. 91–93) 30, 31, 32 support Historian A's viewpoint; 27, 30 support Historian B's viewpoint.

Lesson 17: What Were Conditions Like for Workers in the Meat-packing Industry around 1900?

Objectives

To evaluate sources of information
To evaluate generalizations
To evaluate comparison reasoning
To identify an author's frame of reference

Teaching Ideas

RATIONALE

This lesson is designed to make students more aware of the ideas they get from reading novels, or watching historical dramas on television. Many students are aware that there is a general difference between fiction and non-fiction but they do not know of the specific differences between them.

In Part I of the lesson students will check the accuracy of the novel *The Jungle* by using other sources to corroborate it. They will also examine the unconscious generalizations they may have made from reading the novel. A person who concludes that Lithuanian workers faced terrible conditions in the Chicago Stockyards district about 1900 may have made a sound conclusion. But many students conclude that conditions for workers in general were terrible in the United States. This is an overgeneralization which is examined in Part II of the lesson.

ADJUSTING THE LESSON

The lesson is built around the students reading *The Jungle*. You could do the lesson without the novel, but it would be awkward to do it that way. Obviously, having students read the whole novel can be a problem, due to time constraints. Here are three options for reading less than the whole novel:

Chapters 1–27 (This stops before Jurgis gets caught up in socialism. All the working and living conditions are described.)

Chapters 1–19 (This stops after Jurgis' wife dies and before he becomes a hobo. All the working and living conditions are described.)

Chapters 1–9 (This stops before some of the political corruption is described and leaves out some of the working and living conditions. Many of the conditions are described, however.)

Another possibility is to read portions of the novel out loud in class.

APPROACHES TO THE LESSON

Begin the lesson by asking students to write a response in their notebooks to the question: What were working and living conditions like for workers about 1900? Tell them to keep their response for reference later.

At this point assign *The Jungle*. If you're going to use the worksheet "How Accurate Is *The Jungle*?" (p. 141 in the student book) distribute it and have students fill in the column under *The Jungle*. If you are not using the worksheet, copy the questions onto another sheet to have students record the information from the novel.

After students have read the novel and completed the written work, ask them to write a new answer to the question: "What were working and living conditions like for workers about 1900?" When they have completed their responses ask for volunteers to read their answers. Then ask them to compare their responses at this point to their earlier responses. Are their views now more positive, about the same, or more negative than they were earlier? Ask if the novel influenced their views of workingmen's lives around the turn of the century. Tell them that the degree to which novels should influence our views of history will be discussed later in the lesson.

Discuss the substance of the novel. How did they like it? How good was it? Other questions that could be discussed are:

   a. What were the effects of capitalism or industrialization on people?

   b. How was family life changed in the novel?

   c. How was government portrayed? Why was government so corrupt?

   d. What were the handicaps of immigrants?

   e. How much control did business have over people's lives? Over government?

   f. How are working conditions portrayed?

   g. What does the author show about labor?

   h. How is nature portrayed?

   i. How are unions portrayed?

   j. What did socialism offer?

   k. What is the author's point of view?

   l. How well are the characters developed or portrayed?

Ask students if they should believe what they read in a novel. How are novels different from other sources of information? Have them read the introductory part of the lesson and the section "Historical Novels" (p. 110), including the two questions at the bottom. Some suggested questions for historical novels are:

1. When was it written?

2. Why was it written?

3. What is the background of the author?

4. How much research did the author of the novel do?

5. How are the characters portrayed?

6. What judgments does the author seem to make?

7. What factual information does the author present which could be verified?

Some suggested places to look to get information on historical novels are:

1. Reviews of the novel—Book Review Digest;

2. Literary criticisms of the novel which might tell the background of the author and why it was written;

3. The forward or introduction to the novel, or the description on the jacket cover;

4. Historical information on the topic of the novel;

5. Historical information on the time in which the novel was written.

Ask students where they could find book reviews and the other information.

Now have students read the introduction and sources in Part I of the lesson and either answer the questions at the end of each source or fill in the right-hand column on the worksheet "How Accurate Is *The Jungle?*" Discuss their answers, or have them discuss their answers in groups of three students.

Another strategy that will save time is to divide the class into five groups, each group taking one of the sources (A–

E) and reporting to the rest of the class the extent to which that source supports the descriptions in *The Jungle*.

Finally, have students read the introduction and Source F in Part II of the lesson and answer the questions. Discuss their answers. Make sure you discuss questions 13 and 16, which focus on one of the main goals of the lesson.

You can have students write an essay on the substance of *The Jungle*, on *The Jungle* as a historical source, or on the lessons they learned about drawing historical conclusions from novels, movies, or television dramas.

Suggested Answers

Answers will be suggested in a cursory fashion for the worksheet. More extensive answers are provided for the questions following each source.

WORKSHEET "HOW ACCU-RATE IS *THE JUNGLE*?"

In the novel *The Jungle*, Upton Sinclair portrays working conditions, living conditions, economic conditions, and political conditions as terrible for Lithuanian workers in the Chicago Stockyard district. The owners of the meat-packing factories controlled everything and exploited their workers. The owners cheated Jurgis and Ona on the sale of the house and paid them starvation wages, forcing the children to work. Workers labored in unsanitary and dangerous conditions, and when Jurgis was injured he was replaced since he was no longer useful to the owners. The workers' families lived in overcrowded, unsanitary conditions which led to disease and death. Pollution was everywhere, as shown in the dump and "Bubbly Creek." The government always sided with the rich at the expense of the poor. Votes were bought in elections, and meat inspectors did not stop the flow of unsanitary meat to the consumers.

Sinclair's point is not any one of these issues in particular, but rather that the whole system of capitalism is corrupt. Capitalism perverts everything—work, housing, politics, human relations, family, traditions (the wedding), the environment, etc. Sinclair's solution to this systemic problem is to change the system to socialism. Only when the workers control the factories can true democracy, opportunity for each person, and individual dignity be achieved.

The other sources show, as will be explained in more detail below, that Sinclair was very biased in his perspective but that many of the conditions he describes in the novel are accurate for Lithuanian workers in the Chicago Stockyards District.

QUESTIONS FOLLOWING EACH SOURCE
SOURCE A—*CLIFF'S NOTES*

1. Upton Sinclair had a very anticapitalist perspective to shape the information he found. The reviews are not very helpful because they are too short, and because they give differing views of the novel. Sinclair was in the Stockyards for seven weeks, which strengthens his case.

SOURCE B—NEILL-REYNOLDS COMMISSION

2. The Neill-Reynolds Report confirms what is written in *The Jungle* about poor lighting and ventilation. It also confirms that many unsanitary practices were followed for both the meat and the workers.

3. The Neill-Reynolds Report does not discuss issues such as living conditions, wages, and corruption in government.

4. The Neill-Reynolds Report is more reliable. Novels do not have to be truthful, just believable, whereas history books or reports are supposed to report what really happened to the best of their authors' knowledge. Truthfulness is a standard of excellence for history, not for fiction. History books and reports are also supposed to give sources for their information whereas novels are not.

SOURCE C—THE SOCIAL PROBLEM AT THE CHICAGO STOCKYARDS.

5. The dissertation gives this support:

a. Living conditions—There was a dump, many streets were not paved, the housing was poor, and the area was unsanitary.

b. Mortality rate—high

c. Poverty—Residents of the Stock Yard District were poor compared to Hyde Park residents—many applied for charity; drinking was a problem; many were out of work; wages were not increasing fast

d. Working conditions—Meat-packing houses were unsanitary, poorly lighted, and dangerous. They used child labor and practiced "speeding up" the line.

e. Economic and political power of the owners—They dominated the economic and political systems.

6. The author is either very liberal or radical so he would sympathize with Upton Sinclair and socialism. (Note his beliefs in I and his summary points in VII.)

7. Table 1

a. The comparison is weakened because Hyde Park is a

much wealthier district than the Stock Yard District. It would have been much better to compare the Stock Yard District to another working class area dominated by unskilled immigrant laborers.

b. Since the information is taken from Reports of the Chicago Department of Health it is a complete sample (100%) of the reported deaths in the two wards. In this sense the generalization is excellent. Some deaths may not have been reported, however. Also the Stock Yards District contains more than one ward and the 29th ward may not represent the whole district well. Hyde Park may also contain more than one ward.

SOURCE D—HOUSING CONDITIONS IN CHICAGO STOCKYARDS

8. This study supports *The Jungle's* portrayal of poor, overcrowded, unsanitary housing and environment. It also confirms that many immigrants lost their homes due to falling behind on mortgage payments, which is what happened to Jurgis in the novel. It does not contradict the novel on any points.

9. The two ethnic neighborhoods studied may or may not represent the other Polish and Lithuanian neighborhoods in the Stock Yard District. We have no way of telling how representative the sample is since we do not know if the blocks studied were random or chosen for specific reasons (for example, they seemed to have the worst conditions). The survey of all the homes is good and provides valuable information about the area. Residents may, however, have minimized bad points and exaggerated good points, or vice versa, either consciously or subconsciously.

SOURCE E—WAGES AND FAMILY BUDGETS

10. The study gives this support to the novel:

a. Wages—It shows that wages in the novel ($17\frac{1}{2}$ cents per hour for Jurgis) were probably accurate, and that there were indeed slack times when workers were underemployed.

b. Family expenses—Lithuanian workers would indeed find it difficult to survive, as happened to Jurgis.

c. Children working—Many families had children work, as happened in the Rudkus family in the novel.

d. Overcrowding—Many homes were overcrowded, as in *The Jungle*.

e. Alcohol abuse—The study confirms that alcohol abuse was a serious problem.

11. Although Table 3 suggests a rate of pay of $12.20 per week for workers (see note at bottom of table), the rate for Lithuanians was lower, as shown in Table 4—around $10.00 per week. This rate is comparable to the rates in the tailor shops in Chicago and packing houses in Kansas City, but the latter tables are for all workers, not immigrants. Thus, the immigrant wages in those other places may have been lower than in the Chicago Stock Yards. The rate in Chicago is lower than the rate for Slavic and South-European immigrants, including Lithuanians, in the steel industry.

12. As shown in the answer to question 11, the unskilled workers in Chicago meat packing made more than some workers in other fields and less than others (steel). The Chicago Stock Yards is not representative of places that did not employ mostly immigrants. Nonimmigrants earned higher wages, as we shall see.

13. We have no information about the author directly, but we know he wrote the study through the University of Chicago. Since sources C, D, and E were all done through the University of Chicago we could reasonably infer that from 1902 to 1914 the University had an active research group interested in the problems of poor people in Chicago and in helping those people. Thus it seems reasonable to say this author is sympathetic to the plight of poor workers. On the other hand, much of the study is statistical, but statistics can be selected to paint a particular picture.

SOURCE F—SLAVIC IMMI-
GRANTS IN STEEL MILLS

14. How accurate is *The Jungle* in describing conditions?

a. Slavic immigrants in the steel mills—Here is the fatal flaw in generalizing from reading this novel. This source shows that most immigrants in the steel mills did not bring their families with them, which made survival here much easier. Thus in the novel, Ona, old Antanas, and young Antanas would not have died because they would not have been in the United States. Moreover, Table 9 shows that immigrants improved their situation significantly the longer they stayed in the country. Thus Jurgis is in the worst possible circumstances—he has his family with him and he has been in the country less than 2 years. The awful things that happened to him and his family did happen to some people but they were not representative of most Lithuanian immigrants or of immigrants in general. It is important that students understand that a novel about a Lithuanian immigrant who had lived in Chicago for 6 years and who was a skilled worker when he brought his family over to the United States would be a very different story. Based on the information in this lesson, it is entirely reasonable to conclude that some immigrants faced intolerable conditions in Chicago. It is not reasonable to conclude that most or all immigrants faced terrible conditions.

b. To draw conclusions about all workers in the steel industry is even more of an overgeneralization. As Source F points out, immigrants got the hardest work and the worst conditions. Nonimmigrants had a much easier time (not that it was easy) and a higher percentage of nonimmigrants were skilled workers.

15. The study gives this support to the novel:

a. Dangerous conditions—The steel industry was just as or more dangerous than the meat-packing industry.

b. Defrauding—Companies took advantage of immigrants by renting beaten-up housing for exorbitant rents, higher than for the American born.

c. Housing conditions—Housing was unsanitary, dilapidated and overcrowded.

d. Government corruption—The government cheated immigrants through fines.

All of these support the portrayal in *The Jungle*.

16. Source F is a secondary source which weakens it, but it is clearly based on a great deal of research and the historian seems to have no reason to lie. That is, he may be more objective than the authors of Sources C, D, and E, and he certainly is more objective than Upton Sinclair.

17. As explained in the answer to question 14, drawing general conclusions from a few characters in a novel or movie involves overgeneralizing. Novels and movies only have a few characters, since characters have to be developed along with the plot. There are no statistics and no claims that these characters represent a whole group of people (workers, immigrants, etc.). We subconsciously make that leap.

This problem of overgeneralizing is compounded by the fact that no source or explanation is provided to show why we should believe the events or characters themselves. We cannot check any research done. Who says the events in the movie "Platoon" are accurate at all? Basically, the filmmaker says, "Trust me." Think of all the ideas about history we have formed uncritically and unconsciously from novels, television, dramas, and movies.

HISTORICAL NOTE

The various spellings for Stock Yards in this lesson (Stock-Yard District, Stock Yard District, Stock Yards District, etc.) reflect usage at the time. We have retained the spelling used by each source and have made no attempt to standardize it.

Lesson 18: What Brought about the Progressive Movement?

Objectives

To identify the main idea
To evaluate evidence
To evaluate cause and effect
To evaluate comparisons
To evaluate debating reasoning
To identify unstated assumptions (in the diagrams about politics)
To put written interpretations into visual form (On Bloom's taxonomy this is the synthesis level of thinking.)

Teaching Ideas

Since this lesson focuses on the causes of the Progressive Movement and the relationship of various groups within the movement, students should have some basic knowledge about the Progressive Era and the muckrakers before starting the lesson.

One way to teach the lesson is to begin with the introductory discussion followed by Interpretation A and question sheet, Interpretation B and question sheet, and Interpretation C and question sheet. Students should discuss their answers in small groups and then the class should discuss that interpretation before moving to the next interpretation.

A second method is to give students all three views at the same time and have the students discuss in small groups which view is strongest and why. Then the whole class would discuss which interpretation is strongest.

Suggested Answers
INTERPRETATION A

1. Main point of Interpretation A—The discovery by the public that business was corrupting politics led to the progressive reforms regulating big business.

2. Reasoning

A. Type: Cause and Effect—Cause (public upset about corruption); effect (reforms passed)

   Question: How well does the argument show the connection between the cause and the effect?

   The argument shows that some of the leaders and newspapers said they were concerned about corruption. How do we know, however, if this was genuine concern which led to reform or just talk to placate the masses? There is no effort made to show that there were reforms made against business. So we do not really know if all this talk led to any changes.

B. Type: Generalization

Question: Is the sample representative, or large enough, to make the conclusion a good one?

The argument brings out evidence that the leaders of the Progressive Movement and the media were concerned about business corruption and generalizes that the whole movement was also concerned. This may not be representative of all the groups in the movement. On the other hand, if the leaders were concerned, then it seems reasonable that many of the average people in the movement were concerned.

3. Progressive Movement

This view seems too simple. Any time someone speaks of "the people" it is probably an over simplification. "The people" are not one monolithic group, but rather, many diverse groups who disagree on many things. Who are these subgroups in the Progressive Movement?

4. Operation of politics: Possible model

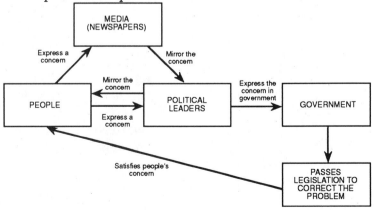

Again this seems too simple. It assumes the media is the prime force in generating reform in society.

5. Evidence in Endnote 1

   It is not too strong. It is public and the authors have reason to distort to make themselves look good.

INTERPRETATION B

6. Main point of Interpretation B—Progressive reforms in the area of business were not an attack on business but rather were designed to help business.

7. Reasoning

A. Type: Debating

   Question: Does this author really weaken the argument of the traditional view?

   This argument is fair (it doesn't use ad hominem, for example) and it does make us question Historian A's argument.

B. Type: Sample

   Question: Is the sample strong enough to make the conclusion a good one?

   The sample in the second paragraph is a more complex view of the Progressive Movement than is found in Historian A. In paragraph 4, sentence 1, we do not know how good the sample is. How many regulatory agencies were controlled by business?

C. Type : Cause and Effect

   Question: How well does the argument show the connection between the cause and the effect?

   The reasoning in the third paragraph is effect-to-cause reasoning. Basically, it argues "The agencies set up by the Progressives helped businessmen. Therefore, those agencies were started by businessmen and professionals, not the poor people." The assumption is that if the poor people started an agency to regulate business, then the agency would not help business that much. But this may not be true. The poorer classes may have initiated the reform, but the businessmen may have later gained control of the agency established by it.

8. Progressive Movement: This view sees the Progressive Movement as comprised of diverse groups with

competing interests. It seems to be a realistic view.

9. Discuss the reasons for students' answers. Did they feel the samples or connections in one view were stronger?

INTERPRETATION C

10. Main point of Interpretation C—Average people were upset by reports of corruption and started reforms to control business.

11. Reasoning

A. Type: Debating

Question: Does the author really weaken the argument of his/her opponent?

This attack on Historian B's view is fair and seems to weaken it significantly. The explanation, for example, that the people may have passed the reforms but the businessmen may have later controlled the reforms makes us rethink one of Historian B's arguments.

B. Type: Comparison

Question: Are the two cases sufficiently different to make the conclusion a good one?

The author argues that the situation in the early 1900s was different enough from the 1800s to account for the progressive reforms in the early 1900s and not earlier. We need some proof that the public really did see the corruption as significantly worse, or that it was due to business size.

C. Type: Cause and Effect

Question: How well does the argument show the connection between the cause and the effect?

The reasoning can be restated in simplified form:

Premise: Progressive business reforms (legislation) occurred right after muckraking articles revealed corruption in government and business.

Premise: Muckraking articles made the public outraged about corruption.

Conclusion: Therefore, progressive business reforms were passed because of the public's outrage about corruption.

This argument does set up a strong correlation between the muckraking articles and the reform legislation. On the other hand, there are several weaknesses in the reasoning. First, the connection between public opinion and the muckrakers is not clearly established. The author seems to assume that the media shapes public opinion or that it reflects public opinion. This assumption may be true for the progressive era, but it should be examined. For example, if polls existed for this time period showing public concern about business corruption, the connection would be much more solidly established.

A second weakness in the reasoning is that it is *post hoc* reasoning ("after, therefore because of"). It is based on the assumption that politicians get involved in issues (the regulations) when the media focuses on those issues. Again this assumption needs to be examined.

While the author shows a significant correlation between the media, public opinion, and progressive business reform, the reasoning does not establish this correlation as a cause. How do we know that the Progressives, controlled by businessmen, did not from the outset pass the reforms for conservative reasons, coincidentally with the muckraking articles?

D. Type: Generalization

Question: Is the sample strong enough to make the conclusion a good one?

In paragraph 5, sentence 1, we would like a bigger

sample than one example to show that "everyone was now concerned about corruption."

In the table, the size and representativeness of the sample of the states is fine. The size of the sample of the legislation is small. It does give us some indication of an increase in regulatory legislation, but it could be special pleading (other types of regulatory legislation may not have increased). The length of time of the sample is short, but we do not know how important this is.

12. Progressive Movement: Possible model

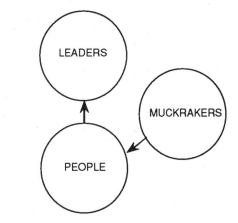

One important question that might arise is: Who are (or who controls) the muckrakers? Why did they write their exposés?

13. Operation of Politics: Possible model—similar to Historian A

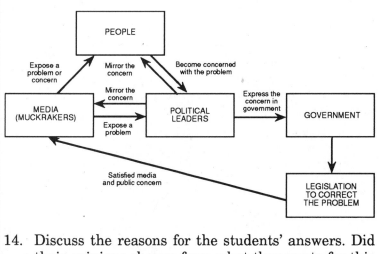

14. Discuss the reasons for the students' answers. Did their opinions change from what they wrote for this same question (#9) under Interpretation B?

UNIT 4
WORKERS, IMMIGRANTS, AND FARMERS
IN THE LATE 1800s

Lesson 19: Assessing the Strengths and Weaknesses of Evidence

Objective

To evaluate evidence

Teaching Ideas

This is a short reinforcement lesson on evaluating evidence. Have students fill in the worksheet, discuss their answers in small groups, and discuss answers as a class. You can save time by skipping the small group work.

Remind students that strength means more reliable and weakness means less reliable. The question we are dealing with is: Can we rely on what this speaker says?

Suggested Answers

	Evidence	Strengths	Weaknesses
1.	Leana	Primary	Reason to lie; cannot check the story (not verifiable); no supporting evidence
2.	Philip	Primary; can check the story	Reason to lie; no supporting evidence given
3.	Lance	Primary; no reason to lie	No supporting evidence
4.	Mill girl	Primary; no reason to lie; private	No supporting evidence; may feel conditions are good because she is hoping they would be good (justify her move to Lowell)
5.	Mill owner	Primary; no reason to lie; private	No supporting evidence
6.	*Lowell Offering*	Primary	Reason to lie; public; no supporting evidence
7.	Henry Frick	Primary (probably)	Reason to lie; public; no supporting evidence
8.	*Encyclopedia Americana*	No reason to lie	Secondary; no supporting evidence
9.	Nurse	No reason to lie; primary	No supporting evidence; public
10.	*Homestead Daily*	None	Reason to lie; secondary (probably); no supporting evidence; public

Lesson 20: Recognizing and Assessing Cause-and-Effect Reasoning

Objectives

To identify cause-and-effect reasoning
To assess the strength of cause-and-effect relationships
To make hypotheses of possible effects

Teaching Ideas

This is a reinforcement lesson on cause-and-effect reasoning. Unlike Lessons 4 and 12, however, it includes a problem (#9) which compares several cause-and-effect arguments on the same point, and it asks students to think of effects on their own.

You could change the lesson by instructing students in Part A to rewrite the items that are not cause and effect (N), so that they become cause-and-effect statements.

After students have individually listed the effects of declining birth rate as asked in question 10, list all their effects on the board. Then have students choose one effect and evaluate the strength of the cause-and-effect reasoning. This assessment of student thinking will help make the skill more personal, and may help transfer it to other areas.

Suggested Answers

1. C Cause—depressed or upset; effect—buys clothes
2. N
3. C Cause—lure of freedom and high wages; effect—immigration to United States
4. N
5. N
6. C Cause—Haymarket Riot; effect—Knights of Labor crippled
7. This argument commits the correlation as cause fallacy (page 6). It argues that the second vice principal caused the discipline problems, when it might very well be that more discipline problems were being punished.
8. This is the same form as problem 7; it commits the correlation as cause fallacy. It is just as likely that immigrants are limited to living in the slum areas. If this hypothesis is correct, then the immigrants were being forced to live in slums, then blamed for the slums!

9. C is the best explanation by far. Students may find this problem very easy. Nevertheless, their explanation of why C is the best answer will reinforce the skill of evaluating cause-and-effect reasoning and will reinforce the standard of excellence in history as to what constitutes a strong cause-and-effect explanation.

Answer A gives no explanation, no cause. It simply restates in a different way that Americans had fewer children. Answer B only gives one explanation for fewer children—children had no economic role. Everything else in the explanation is irrelevant. Answer D gives explanations of why people married earlier in life, but not why they had fewer children. Answer C shows that less economic role, more time required to rear children, and desire for consumption of products all led to the lower birthrate.

10. Possible effects
    - Close relationships between parents and children;
    - Sexual tensions between husbands and wives (without common use of birth control, the only way to reduce birth rates was abstinence);
    - Longer life expectancy for women (childbirth was a major killer of women);
    - Tension about the role of women (with fewer children, what were they supposed to do with their time?);
    - More free time for parents; more parental time devoted to each child;
    - More attention to children's needs; big time toy industry; books on raising children;
    - Changing demographic patterns as this smaller population of children gets older, i.e., lower demand for homes when they become adults, fewer taxpayers, etc.;
    - More reliance on pension funds.

Lesson 21: Recognizing and Evaluating Types of Reasoning

Objectives

To identify and evaluate comparisons
To identify and evaluate generalizations
To identify and evaluate cause and effect

Teaching Ideas

This lesson is a reinforcement lesson on identifying and evaluating types of reasoning. If the skill needs to be broken down into parts, see the teacher's guide for Lesson 13. In this lesson, students must remember to identify the types of reasoning, ask the correct questions, and then make their judgments without any prompts. You can make the lesson less difficult by giving the students prompts.

If necessary, have students do Problem 1 and discuss it as a class. Ask if students have any questions about how to fill in the sheet. Have students fill in the rest of the sheet, discuss their answers in small groups, and discuss the group answers as a class.

Suggested Answers

1. Immigrants—This is primarily a cause-and-effect argument (it is also a generalization and a comparison). It explains the connection between the cause and the effect to some extent, but it is incomplete. For example, a larger demand for workers may have led to increased immigration. Also, there might be other causes for lower wages, such as depression or general deflation.

2. Workers—This is primarily a comparison (it is also a generalization). The key question is: How are the two cases (time periods in this example) similar and different? The working conditions comparison seems fine, since the definition of good working conditions probably did not change much. The wages comparison might be weak if prices rose more than wages did (an important difference). Workers may, in fact, be worse off despite higher wages.

3. This is primarily cause-and-effect reasoning (it is also a generalization). The connection between famine and emigration is not explained, but it makes sense. Other factors, such as job opportunities, may have caused emigration also. It may be that the potato

famine was the main cause of emigration, but this person should explain how it was the main cause.

4. This is primarily a generalization. We would like to know what kind of sample was used to make this generalization. Since we do not know the sample, we cannot really evaluate the argument.

5. This is primarily cause and effect. It explains the connection between the cause and the effect in a simplistic way. It does not consider other possible causes for corrupt bosses.

6. This is primarily a generalization. The part about strikes is unclear. How many strikes were in the sample? How many is enough to show workers' willingness to fight? The part about few strikes being successful may also be based on a poor sample, but it would be relatively easy to look up the outcomes of various strikes.

Lesson 22: Identifying and Evaluating Proof and Debating Reasoning

Objectives

To identify and evaluate proof by evidence or example
To identify and evaluate proof by authority
To identify and evaluate debating or eliminating alternatives

Teaching Ideas

This is a straightforward lesson on practicing evaluating proof and debating reasoning. Make sure students read over the explanations on pages 11–14 of the student book before beginning the problems. They should note especially the cue words, questions to ask, and fallacies. Have them fill in the worksheet, compare answers in small groups, and discuss their answers as a class. If necessary, do the first problem or two as a class, then have the students fill in the rest of the sheet on their own.

Suggested Answers

1. E The evidence does not show that medical care is getting better. This is the irrelevant proof fallacy, page 12.

2. D If there was, in fact, no one else at home besides Marie and the author, then the conclusion is fine.

3. A Since the two professors are in sociology, it is reasonable to argue that they are experts on housing conditions. They might not be the foremost experts and we might want to check their credentials further.

4. E This evidence does prove the point. This is also authoritative so a student could legitimately answer A.

5. D This is a legitimate, if debatable, criticism of Sumner's views.

6. D This is the attacking the arguer fallacy, page 14.

7. E This is the prevalent proof ("everyone knows") fallacy, page 12.

8. D The workers did have alternatives to the use of force, such as continuing to strike, boycotting, or trying to publicize what Frick was doing. The alternatives may not have been very desirable but we do not know that.

9. E or A This is the numbers fallacy, page 12.

10. D This is the golden mean fallacy, page 13.

Lesson 23: What Were American Cities Like in the Late 1800s?

Objectives

To use evidence to support an argument
To evaluate evidence
To evaluate generalizations

Teaching Ideas

This lesson is divided into two parts, each of which is a topic for debate on American cities. After students are assigned one of the debate topics, they must figure out which information can be used to support their side of the debate. Have them debate in small groups and then as a class, with half the students debating while the rest listen. Encourage students to question the reliability of sources.

Alternatively, you could use the information from the lesson as a starter, to be supplemented by further research.

Follow up the lesson by having students write an essay answering the debate topic they were assigned. The debate topics are:

> Part I—On balance, were urban bosses good for American cities in the late 1800s?

> Part II—On balance, were American cities healthy places to live in the late 1800s?

Suggested Breakdown of Information

PART I

Informational/Neither side—1, 2

Affirmative (Bosses were good)—4, 5, 7, 8, 12, 13, 15, 16

Negative (Bosses were bad)—3, 6, 9, 10, 11, 14, 17, 18

PART II

Informational—19

Affirmative (Cities were healthy)—21, 22, 25, 27, 30, 31, 33

Negative (Cities were not healthy)—20, 23, 24, 26, 28, 29, 32

Lesson 24: What Was the Town of Pullman Like?

Objectives

To find the main point
To identify unstated assumptions
To evaluate evidence
To evaluate proof reasoning
To evaluate generalizations
To evaluate cause and effect
To evaluate debate reasoning
To evaluate comparison reasoning

Teaching Ideas

This lesson has students analyze two opposing viewpoints on the town of Pullman during the time period leading up to the Pullman Strike of 1894.

Begin by asking students why the owner of a company might build a town for his workers. List the possible reasons on the chalkboard. Tell them this involves the question of "motives," and that the question of why a company owner set up a town for his workers is part of the problem with which they will be dealing. Ask if anyone has heard the term "paternalism" and have someone look it up.

Have students read the two interpretations noting a particular number of strengths and weaknesses. (For example, "Evaluate two points of reasoning and two pieces of evidence in each interpretation.") Ask students to discuss their analyses in small groups and have each group make a report to the class. You can provide more structure by having students fill in the worksheet "Subquestions on the Town of Pullman" (p. 176).

Alternatively, have students read the two interpretations and answer the questions on pages 171–75. Or you could have a debate on the conditions in the town of Pullman.

You can make the lesson less difficult by focusing on the evidence in the interpretations, and not dealing with assumptions or reasoning.

This is a fairly high interest lesson. Some students may tire of a detailed analysis, however, especially of assumptions and types of reasoning. If you anticipate that your students will be bored with the worksheets, have them discuss or debate the viewpoints.

Suggested Answers

INTERPRETATION A

1. Main point of Interpretation A—George Pullman oppressed his workers and provoked the Pullman Strike. Also, George Pullman's greedy policies caused the Pullman Strike.

2. Assumption

   Pullman forced the newspaper, businesses, and public institutions to take anti-union positions.

3. Analysis of reasoning

Paragraph	Type of Reasoning	Key Question(s)	Your Evaluation (How well answered— Any fallacies?)
Paragraph 2, Sentences 3–7	Proof by evidence	Does the evidence prove the point?	The evidence indicates excessive profits. (How strong the evidence itself is will be dealt with in the section on evidence.)
	Generalization	Is the sample representative?	It could be stronger. Are these all the expenses of running the town? Over what time period was the sample done?
Paragraph 2, Sentence 8	Proof ("It makes sense....")	Does the argument prove the point?	It does not prove the point, but if the premise (he had a monopoly) is true, then it does make sense that he could make unusually large profits.
Paragraph 4, Sentence 2 (including Endnote 6)	Generalization	Is the sample representative?	There is only one case to prove the whole generalization. We need more than this.
	Proof by evidence	Does the evidence prove the point?	
Paragraph 5, Sentence 7 (including Endnote 10)	Proof (He uses the evidence of profits to prove that Pullman did not have to cut wages.)	Does the evidence prove the point?	This evidence does seem to lead to the conclusion that Pullman should not have cut wages. How good the evidence itself is will be dealt with in the section on evidence.
Paragraph 6	Cause and Effect (Pullman forced or caused the workers to join the ARU and to go on strike.)	Does the author show the connection between the cause and the effect?	Did Pullman's intransigence cause the workers to join the ARU and to strike or did the workers joining the ARU cause Pullman's intransigence? The argument rests on whether Pullman actually had to cut wages and whether he fired the three workers because they were in the union.

4. Evidence in endnote 5

   P— Not sure if primary or secondary—if the newspaper had a reporter at the announcement, then it is primary.

   R— The newspaper had a reason to distort. (One gets the impression from the number of times that the *Chicago Times* is used to support Historian A, and from what is contained in the quotes, that the paper was sympathetic to the strikers.) Parend had no reason to distort. This is the key.

O— No other evidence supporting this evidence.

P— Public

This evidence seems very strong. If Parend did say this, then it is very likely that the company was, in fact, kicking strikers out of town. We must, however, try to get another source on what Parend said to see if the paper distorted the intention of the statement.

INTERPRETATION B

5. Main point of Interpretation B—George Pullman was good to his workers, but his workers went on the unprovoked strike anyway.

6. Assumption

There is no way for someone to control elections if citizens vote by secret ballot. (This is worth discussing.)

7. Analysis of reasoning

Paragraph	Type of Reasoning	Key Question(s)	Your Evaluation (How well answered— Any fallacies?)
Paragraph 2	Debating ("Some people have alleged....")	Does the author seriously weaken the other argument?	The evidence presented here certainly makes one wonder about the other viewpoint.
	Proof by evidence	Does the evidence prove the point?	It looks good, but statistics can certainly be used in a distorted way.
Paragraph 6	Cause and Effect (The depression caused Pullman to cut wages.)	Does the author show the connection between the cause and the effect?	It is logical that the depression might force a pay cut, but 25%—40%? We need to see profit rates for the company to know if the depression was a sufficient cause, or whether it was used as an excuse by Pullman to cut costs.
Paragraph 7	Debating ("Some people say....")	Does the author seriously weaken the other argument?	Not too well. It seems that if the town was established for the good of the company and its workers, then it could be run at a loss for the overall good of the company.
	Comparison	Are the two cases really dissimilar (in this argument)?	They are not that separate. Pullman owns them both and they are interrelated. Pullman could have run the town at a loss.
Paragraph 8, sentences 3 and 4 (including Endnote 11)	Proof by evidence	Does the evidence prove the point?	Because it was only 3 workers out of 43 on the committee does not necessarily mean that the workers were not fired because of their union affiliation nor does the denial by subordinate company officials that they knew the workers were on the committee.
	Generalization	Is the sample representative?	
	Cause and Effect	Does the author show the connection?	

8. Evidence in endnote 8

P— Primary

R— He has every reason to distort this statement to justify his actions.

O— There is no other evidence to support this evidence. It would be easy to find out if there was a depression, so it is likely that there was one. The depression, however, did not necessarily justify a pay cut or such a large pay cut.

P— It is public.

Overall, this evidence is weak. Pullman is not a reliable source on why he cut wages.

General Questions

9. Compare endnote 1 (Interpretation A) with endnote 2 (Interpretation B).

P— Wickes' statement is primary, while Carwardine's is probably second hand.

R— Wickes has an obvious reason to distort, and distortion is possible with statistics. Carwardine may not be very objective either, as all his statements are pro union.

O— There is no other evidence supporting either statement. Both (the costs and charges for water) could be checked on, however, which increases their reliability.

P— Both are public statements which weakens them.

There are several ways to decide which is stronger. One possibility to consider is that both men are telling the truth. In this case Wickes accounts for Carwardine's explanation and shows that even at those prices the company made very little money.

10. Compare endnote 6 (Interpretation A) with endnote 5 (Interpretation B).

Both are primary and public statements and neither is supported by other evidence. The company pamphlet has much less reliability than the statement by the tenant because the company has every reason to exaggerate the good points of the town, and gloss over the bad points. On the other hand, the tenant talks about only one family, so even if his statement is true, it does not show that the whole town was a bad place to live.

11. Compare endnote 12 (Interpretation A) with endnote 10 (Interpretation B).

    It is conclusive that it was Pullman who refused to arbitrate. Whether he had good reason to refuse is a matter of opinion.

12. See the answer for question 9, but students should also consider endnotes 3 and 4 for Historian B in their assessment.

13. Both interpretations agree that rents in the town were higher than in neighboring towns. See the answer for question 10 for an assessment of evidence on living conditions in the town.

14. The evidence in Historian A, endnote 10 is damaging to Pullman. Students must decide if making a profit while cutting wages and squeezing workers by keeping rents the same is justified.

15. Paragraph 3, endnote 3 from Historian A shows that there would have been pressure on workers to live in the town. Historian B (paragraph 4) countered that the secret ballot would limit Pullman's control.

16. See the answer for question 10.

Lesson 25: Should the United States Restrict Immigration?

Objectives

To find the main point
To evaluate evidence
To evaluate proof reasoning
To evaluate cause and effect
To evaluate generalizations
To evaluate comparison reasoning
To identify unstated assumptions

Teaching Ideas

This lesson focuses on arguments for and against restricting immigration in the early 1900s. It deals with the wave of immigration from roughly 1870 to 1920. The next lesson deals with the actual restrictions by focusing on the quota acts passed in the 1920s.

You could begin by having students fill in and discuss the "Survey on Immigration" (page 184). This will get them thinking about the immigration issue today. Tell them that now we will focus on earlier immigration.

The strategy envisioned at this point is to have students read Historian A and evaluate it before seeing Historian B, which gives away some of the weaknesses in Historian A. It should be noted that the real historian from whom Historian A's argument was written actually made much more complex arguments on several points. He recognized, for example, that immigrant poverty was largely due to conditions in the United States and that immigrant crime was partly due to the larger percentage of adult males in their population. The historian's arguments were simplified to help students pick out weaknesses in arguments.

After students have answered the questions for Historian A, have them discuss the answers in small groups and then as a class. Repeat this format for Historian B.

Alternative strategies are: (a) have students evaluate the viewpoints according to the ARMEAR model (p. 18); (b) have a class discussion on the question of immigration restriction; (c) have a debate based on the two viewpoints.

Question 4 under Historian A is a very interesting problem. It involves the relevant information and an understanding of some basic economics. If you feel your students may not grasp the economics necessary to answer this question you might want to have them read the explanation "Circular Flow Diagram" (p. 183). Remind the students to look at the relevant information.

Suggested Answers

Historian A .

1. Main point of Historian A—Restrict immigration.

2. This is an interesting paragraph! There are three weaknesses in the paragraph. Firstly, the second sentence is the prevalent proof fallacy, page 12. Secondly, the third sentence commits the fallacy of begging the question (not included in the "Guide to Critical Thinking"). In this fallacy, the premise, after it is reworded, is the same as the conclusion. In this case the simplified argument is: premise—immigrants come to improve their standard of living (because they are poor); conclusion—therefore, immigrants are poor. Thirdly, the last sentence is a stereotype (page 11) of large groups of Europeans.

3. This is a cause-and-effect argument. If immigrants are indeed willing to work for lower wages, they might lower the wages of American workers. They also might take the worst jobs, however, moving American workers up to higher paid jobs. Relevant Information A and F show other possible causes for lower wages.

4. An evaluation of these two sentences involves looking at the relevant information. This argument is based on the assumption that immigrants take jobs but do not create jobs. But all people (including immigrants) consume products, so immigrants must create jobs to make those products. (See Relevant Information D) The question is whether immigrants create more jobs than they take. The "Circular Flow Diagram" sheet may help some students understand this principle of job creation. Also, Relevant Information C shows that lower wages may actually have caused a decrease of unemployment.

5. The argument on pauperism is the fallacy of composition, page 10. The whole group (all people living in America, native and immigrant) has a lower standard of living on average when poor people are added to the population. (They lower the average.) But American-born workers may not be any worse off—they may have a higher standard of living. When the slave population doubles, the *average* standard of living of a slave society goes down (there are more people averaged into the total who have no wealth), but the slave *owners* have a higher standard of living.

6. This argument involves an unfair comparison which can be figured out by looking at Relevant Information B, E, and G. The most crime-prone part of the immigrant group (adult males) is being compared to the average of the native group (men, women, and children). Naturally, the immigrant rate is higher. A fair argument would have compared adult male immigrants to American-born adult males. This argument shows more crime by immigrants, but it does not prove that something in the racial character of immigrants causes them to commit crimes, as argued in endnote 2.

7. The Commission assumes that immigrants are racially inferior and that insanity is at least partly caused by genetically determined racial traits.

HISTORIAN B

8. Main point of Historian B—Immigration should not be restricted.

9. This is debating and it looks like a fair criticism of Historian A's argument.

10. This is a comparison of population increase to employment increase. It does not matter why the jobs increased faster than population, since in any case immigrant workers would not have been taking jobs from Americans. (There were other jobs opening up.) So the comparison is a good one.

11. The main type of reasoning is generalization. What specifically does "generally" mean? A majority? Almost all? A sizeable number? We also want to know how large a sample this historian looked at to make this generalization.

12. In these sentences Historian B offers a different cause than did Historian A for the lower standard of living in the United States.

13. Again Historian B offers a different cause than did Historian A. It is hard to say which cause is more important but we see more possibilities now than we did after reading Historian A only.

OVERALL

14. Historian B's argument is probably stronger, based on the numerous weaknesses in Historian A's case.

Lesson 26: Why Was the Immigration Act of 1924 Passed?

Objectives

To analyze primary sources
To make inferences
To write an interpretation
To analyze graphs and cartoons
To relate information to hypotheses

Teaching Ideas

Begin this lesson by telling the class that Congress severely restricted immigration into the United States in 1924. Ask: "Why do you think some Americans wanted to restrict immigration?" List student answers on the board.

Have students write a 100-word explanation of why the Immigration Act was passed, as directed in the student book at the beginning of the lesson. Cue students to look especially at the change in dates used in determining immigration quotas. Remind them to piece information together from several documents, and to look at symbols in the cartoons.

After students have finished writing their explanations, break up the class into small groups and ask each group to discuss why the Immigration Act was passed and then write an explanation based on the group discussion. Have the groups read their reports aloud, and discuss their conclusions as a class.

Follow up the lesson by having students take their original explanations home, marked up now with notes from the discussion. They should make whatever changes they think are appropriate, based on the discussion, and re-write their explanations into polished final essays. Have them pass in the rough draft (first explanation) with the final copy.

Suggested Points of Emphasis

The date for determining quotas was moved from 1910 to 1890 to restrict immigrants from Southern and Eastern Europe, as shown on the graphs in Document B. Farmers and patriotic groups, made up mostly of descendants of early immigrants of Anglo-Saxon origin, and labor unions were in favor of the bill, showing economic, nationalistic, and racial motives. An emphasis on racial superiority is stated explicitly in the South Carolina senator's speech (Document D). Fear of foreign ideas, especially communism and anarchy, is shown in the cartoon labeled Document E. Fear of being swamped by the foreigners is shown in the cartoon labeled Document F. The belief in the racial inferiority of Southern and Eastern Europeans is shown in Document G.

Lesson 27: What Does the Omaha Platform Show about the Populists?

Objectives

To evaluate a primary source
To use relevant information
To identify unstated assumptions
To make inferences

Teaching Ideas

This lesson focuses on making inferences and identifying assumptions by having students look at the Omaha Platform. It is better to have students do this lesson before having them read about the Populists. If they know about the Populists first they can answer the questions from memory—they will not be forced to infer them by looking at the Omaha Platform.

Have students read the introduction and ask them what a party platform is. Have them read the Omaha Platform and answer questions 1–17, then have them read the relevant information and answer the rest of the questions. They can discuss their answers in small groups and then as a class. You can make the lesson easier by doing 2 or 3 problems as a class first, then having students work in pairs on the others. You can shorten the lesson by focusing on only some of the questions.

Conclude the lesson by asking students, "With which of the Populist suggestions do you agree?" You might want to focus on IV, VII, IX, XII, and XV. These proposals will make students wrestle with the issue of the proper role of government in a democratic society. This theme can be picked up later in the course in the Progressive Movement, 1920s, New Deal, 1960s, and 1980s as the country went through liberal and conservative political philosophies.

EXTENDING THE LESSON

There are a number of ways to extend the lesson. Students could write an essay on the beliefs of the Populists. They could look up which of the suggested Populist reforms were later adopted. Or some of the students could read about the Populists in Chapters I–III of *The Age of Reform* by Richard Hofstadter.

Suggested Answers

A. While there are many reasonable inferences that can and should be drawn from the Omaha Platform, there is room for differences of opinion on a number of the questions. What appears here are some suggested lines of reasoning. As in the other lessons in these books, the emphasis is more on the thinking which the students do rather than on the answers they choose.

	Statement	Check	Reason
1	Rich people deserve to keep the money they have.	No	II, VII—graduated income tax
2	Immigration is bad for the country.	Yes	IX, X—seem to indicate this
3	Speculators hurt other people, such as farmers.	Yes	IX
4	Business owners make an important contribution to creating wealth through the production of goods and services.	No	II
5	There is fraud or intimidation of voters in elections.	Yes	XII
6	Wealth should be more equally divided.	Yes	VII
7	Society can be improved through reform.	Yes	This whole platform is intended as a reform. Would they try it if they thought reform was impossible?
8	The people should have more say in government.	Yes	XII, XIII, XIV
9	Reform can be achieved through the Democratic and Republican parties.	No	The introduction attacks the two parties as having allowed the situation to get this bad. They caused the problem.
10	Freedom is more important than equality.	No	The platform indicates that inequality of wealth and power is threatening to ruin our country. By imposing more equality of wealth (VII) and power (IV, VIII, IX, XII, XIII, XIV, XV) the situation will be largely corrected. In the process "the people" will also achieve more freedom—they were controlled by the rich before. These proposals in the platform will limit the freedom of the rich and powerful in order to gain more equality.
11	An important aspect of history is the struggle between the rich and the poor.	Yes	The introduction says there are rich and poor classes. I and III say the poor should unite against their enemy (the rich).
12	The state legislatures are controlled by the rich people.	Yes	XIV indicates that something is wrong with the state legislatures picking the Senators. It seems reasonable to infer from the statements about the rich controlling so much that this is what the Populists think is the problem with the state legislatures choosing the Senators.
13	It is possible for a conspiracy of a small number of people to control the history of a country for a time.	Yes	It seems from the introduction and statements III and V that the Populists believe that a small number of rich people, probably bankers, have conspired to control the country. The question of whether the Populists were anti-Semitic could be discussed here.
14	The government is controlled by the rich—it must be reformed.	Yes	XII, XIII, XIV, and the introduction
15	Bankers have too much power.	Yes	V

B. Based on the Omaha Platform and the relevant information, put a check next to the statements which you think are probably true. Write the reason you checked or did not check each statement.

	Statement	Check	Reason
16	Many farmers were debtors (they owed money on loans).	Yes	VI, Relevant Information A, C, E
17	Farmers felt railroads were hurting them.	Yes	IV, Relevant Information B
18	The Populists were trying to gain the support of industrial workers.	Yes	I, II, III, X, XI, Relevant Information F
19	Bankers supported the idea of free coinage of silver.	No	VI, Relevant Information A, D
20	Populists were conservative.		This could be an interesting discussion. The idea of government involvement in the economy in the name of the people was radical for that time period, but not radical today. Some historians (such as Richard Hofstadter) thought that the Populists were conservative in that they wanted to go back to the golden age of farming when the yeoman farmer was looked upon with dignity, rather than taken advantage of by the forces of industrialization. You might want to read about the Populists in <u>The Age of Reform</u> by Hofstadter. Another interesting point is what is meant by radical. Government ownership of business is radical to many students, but many of the other Populist suggestions are accepted today as ordinary, not radical.
21	Populists were radical.		

C. Why didn't the Populists win? Listen to their hypotheses. Remind students that although the Populists did not win the election, many of their suggestions were later adopted in our government (secret ballot, initiative, referendum, graduated income tax, direct election of senators, shorter work week).

PART I—INDIVIDUAL SKILLS

Identifying Evidence

 Label each item below with the appropriate letter.

> **S** A **source** of information is given.
>
> **N** **No** source of information is given.

_____1. The black codes made the Northern representatives in Congress angry.

_____2. In reaction to the Union Leagues, which helped achieve Republican control of the South, Southerners formed secret organizations to fight back.

_____3. The Republican Party platform of 1876 stated that the Republicans pledged to protect the rights of all citizens in the South.

_____4. Historian Kenneth Stampp argued in his book on Reconstruction that the Radical Republicans were sincerely interested in helping blacks in the South.

_____5. Everyone knows that physical violence by Southern whites helped overthrow the radical governments in the South.

Evaluating Evidence

 In the space provided, use at least three of the criteria you learned in class to evaluate the following evidence.

A. The renter told the landlord that she did not do the damage to the apartment. She said someone broke into the apartment and tore up the place, so she shouldn't be charged for the repairs.

6. Strengths:

7. Weaknesses:

[Continued on next page.]

[Continued from previous page.]

B. William Dunning, a white historian from the South, says in his book that the failure of Reconstruction was not the fault of Southern whites. He says the Northern Radicals went overboard in controlling the South, which caused all the problems.

    8. Strengths:

    9. Weaknesses:

C. In his book, *History of the Labor Movement in the United States* (1970), historian Philip Foner says that working conditions at Homestead Steel were very poor.

    10. Strengths:

    11. Weaknesses:

D. The commissioners of labor of the State of Illinois made a report on labor conditions in 1893. In it they stated that, based on the company records, workers at the Pullman plant who did not live in the town of Pullman were fired first.

    12. Strengths:

[Continued on next page.]

[Continued from previous page.]

   13. Weaknesses:

E.   Eugene V. Debs, leader of the strikers at Pullman in 1894, stated in a newspaper article in the *Chicago Times* in April 1894, "I will negotiate at any time with Mr. Pullman."

   14. Strengths:

   15. Weaknesses:

F.   Factory owner Peter Thomas tells a newspaper reporter that he admits he is not paying his workers enough wages on which to survive.

   16. Strengths:

   17. Weaknesses:

[Continued on next page.]

[Continued from previous page.]

Identifying Cause-and-Effect Reasoning

 Label each item below with the appropriate letter.

C-E The item involves **cause-and-effect** reasoning.

N The item does **not** involve cause-and-effect reasoning.

_____18. J.P. Morgan was one of the richest men in America in 1907.

_____19. Large machines changed the way work was done in America.

_____20. People reacted to Rockefeller's monopoly in oil by trying to get the government to regulate business.

_____21. Prices for farm products declined significantly in the late 1800s.

Evaluating Cause-and-Effect Reasoning

 Evaluate the following cause-and-effect arguments by filling in the boxes and answering the questions.

22. Many Americans in the late 1800s wanted to restrict immigration to the "desirable" people. This led Congress to pass a literacy test requirement for immigrants, so that immigration would be limited to people who could read or write.

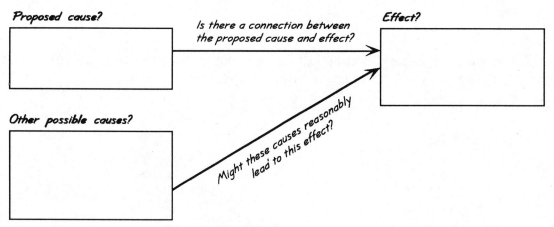

Overall, how strong is this reasoning?

[Continued on next page.]

[Continued from previous page.]

23. The new mighty corporations, such as US Steel and Standard Oil, alarmed many Americans. The corporations were richer and more powerful than any state government.

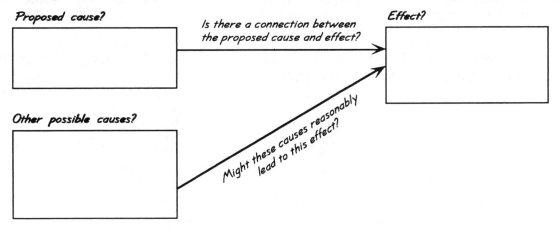

Overall, how strong is this reasoning?

Identifying Comparisons

Q Label each item below with the appropriate letter.

    C   The item involves **comparison** reasoning.

    N   The item does **not** involve comparison reasoning.

_____24. The average American was better off in 1900 than in 1865.

_____25. Textile production increased dramatically after the invention of the power loom.

_____26. Reconstruction legislatures were corrupt. Their misuse of public funds was astonishing.

[Continued on next page.]

[Continued from previous page.]

Evaluating Comparisons

 Evaluate the following comparison arguments. Tell whether the comparison is strong or weak and explain why you think so.

27.   The 1980s was another Gilded Age for American Society. The rich got richer and the poor got poorer in both time periods.

28.   Blacks were probably better off under slavery than they were as freedmen in the 1870s. At least in slavery they were guaranteed food, clothing, and shelter by their masters.

Identifying Generalizations

 Label each of the following with the appropriate letter.

G   The item involves **generalization** reasoning.

N   The item does **not** involve generalization reasoning.

_____29.   Most Southerners allowed the violence against blacks to continue because of their racism toward blacks.

_____30.   The Republicans overrode President Johnson's veto of the Civil Rights Bill.

_____31.   President Johnson vetoed the Civil Rights Bill.

_____32.   Henry Frick refused to talk with the union leader during the Homestead Strike.

[Continued on next page.]

[Continued from previous page.]

Evaluating Generalizations

 Evaluate the following generalizations. Make sure you make an overall judgment (strong or weak) about each argument.

33. State debts increased in all the Southern states under the Republican governments.

34. Steel workers in the late 1800s had very dangerous working conditions. In the Homestead plant (factory), for example, there were many accidents in the 1890s.

Identifying Unstated Assumptions

 Write the letter of the unstated assumption.

"The Radical Republicans were evil men. After all, they wanted to restrict the rights of Southern white political leaders."

_____35. What is the unstated assumption?

A. People who restrict the rights of political leaders are evil.

B. Evil men always restrict the rights of political leaders.

C. Republicans are evil.

D. Political leaders who have their rights restricted are good.

[Continued on next page.]

[Continued from previous page.]

"Chuck comes from a rich family. His father drives a Cadillac."

_____36.   What is the unstated assumption?

A. Chuck is rich.

B. People who are rich drive Cadillacs.

C. People who drive Cadillacs are rich.

D. People who don't drive a Cadillac are not rich.

E. Chuck can drive his father's car.

Identifying Types of Reasoning

 Identify the type of reasoning in each of the following by writing the letter of the correct answer.

A—Comparison	C—Cause and effect
B—Generalization	D—Proof by Authority

_____37.   The mistreatment of Southern whites by Northern Republicans resulted in the South voting solidly for the Democratic party thereafter.

_____38.   During Reconstruction whites still controlled most state legislatures in the South. In Alabama, whites outnumbered blacks 58 to 26. In Florida, whites outnumbered blacks 214 to 32.

_____39.   Jane had been successful because of her hard work and her honesty.

_____40.   Andrew Carnegie may have been well known for his fortune, but John D. Rockefeller was much richer. Rockefeller had over $1 billion.

_____41.   Railroads in the late 1800s were built hastily.

_____42.   According to the respected historian, Allan Nevins, Rockefeller was an honest and sincere businessman.

PART II—MIXED PROBLEMS

Two students (Joan and Harold) are debating the 19th-century idea of Social Darwinism. Specifically, they are debating whether the rich deserve to be rich and the poor deserve to be poor.

I. Joan: The rich are the fittest. It's like Darwin's theory of survival of the fittest in nature. Only the fittest survive.

[Continued on next page.]

[Continued from previous page.]

II. Harold: The poor work hard. The rich don't work hard, many are born into their wealth.

III. Joan: Animals all work hard and many don't survive. If you're unfit you won't survive whether or not you try hard.

IV. Harold: Are you saying the rich are physically superior to the poor?

V. Joan: No.

VI. Harold: Are a rabbit and bear equal?

VII. Joan: They may have been at one point but developed differently.

VIII. Harold: Many rich are born into wealth. They have all the advantages so the poor can't compete with them.

IX. Joan: The poor can become rich if they try. Andrew Carnegie was an example of rags to riches. That shows that the poor can become rich.

X. Harold: Carnegie got help from a rich person to become rich. Getting rich is like playing poker—it's luck. Luck doesn't mean you're fit or that you deserve wealth.

XI. Joan: The lucky are more fit to survive.

Questions on the Debate

_____43.   What is the conclusion to argument I?

A. The rich are the fittest.

B. Only the fittest survive.

C. It's like Darwin's theory of survival of the fittest.

D. The rich deserve to be rich, the rich deserve to survive.

_____44.   What type of reasoning is primarily used in argument I?

A. Analogy (comparison)

B. Generalization

C. Cause and Effect

D. Proof by Authority

_____45.   What is the conclusion of argument II?

A.   The poor work hard.

B. The rich don't work hard.

C. Many rich are born into their wealth.

D. The rich don't deserve to be rich.

[Continued on next page.]

[Continued from previous page.]

_____46.　What is an unstated assumption in argument II?

A.　The poor work hard.

B.　People who don't work hard don't deserve their wealth.

C.　Being born into wealth is fine.

D.　The rich give some of their wealth to private charities.

_____47.　What is Harold doing in argument IV?

A.　Questioning evidence.

B.　Disagreeing with Joan's value position.

C.　Clarifying similarities and differences in Joan's comparison.

D.　Questioning the representativeness of Joan's sample.

_____48.　What type of reasoning is primarily used in the second sentence in argument X?

A.　Analogy

B.　Generalization

C.　Cause and Effect

D.　Proof by Authority

Some words are hard to pin down. For example, if you told me someone else is a good basketball player, I'd have a hard time deciding if you're right because what you think of as good may not be good to me. So the word *good* is difficult to define.

_____49.　Which word from the debate would cause the greatest definitional problem?

A.　Nature

B.　Poker

C.　Survival

D.　Poor

_____50.　Which word from the debate would cause the greatest definitional problem?

A.　Lucky

B.　Animals

C.　Fittest

D.　Evolved

　©1991 Midwest Publications/Critical Thinking Press & Software, P.O. Box 448, Pacific Grove, CA　93950

TEST QUESTION ANSWERS

Teaching Ideas

As mentioned in the introduction, students should be evaluated in a variety of ways, not just by objective tests. So although fifty test items are included in the *Teacher's Guide*, you should also consider evaluating students using problems from the student text. One of the best evaluation methods is to give students an interpretation you haven't analyzed in class and have them write an evaluation of it. You could supply the criteria for evaluation, such as finding the main idea, identifying and evaluating two pieces of evidence, identifying and evaluating two types of reasoning, identifying one assumption, bringing in any relevant information on the topic, and making an overall judgment.

The fifty items on the test are meant to examine student mastery of the skills listed on the scope and sequence chart on pages 12–13, primarily identifying and evaluating evidence, cause-and-effect reasoning, comparison reasoning, generalization reasoning, and identifying unstated assumptions.

Suggested Answers

IDENTIFYING EVIDENCE

Part I Individual skills

1. N
2. N
3. S   The Republican Party platform
4. S   Kenneth Stampp
5. N

EVALUATING EVIDENCE

A. Renter

   6. Strengths: Primary source

   7. Weaknesses: Reason to lie; no other evidence that someone else broke into the apartment

B. Dunning

   8. Strengths: He's an expert, a historian.

   9. Weaknesses: Secondary source; reason to lie; no other evidence

C. Foner

   10. Strengths: He's an expert; no reason to lie

   11. Weaknesses: Secondary source; no other evidence

D. Commissioners

12. Strengths: Looked at primary sources; the company records are support for their claim.

13. Weaknesses: Secondary source; the commissioners may have been against the Pullman Company but we're not sure.

E. Debs

14. Strengths: He's a primary source.

15. Weaknesses: Debs may be saying he'll negotiate, while he secretly makes it impossible to negotiate; he has a reason to lie; no other evidence.

F. Thomas

16. Strengths: Primary source; no reason to lie

17. Weaknesses: No other evidence

IDENTIFYING CAUSE-AND-EFFECT REASONING

18. N
19. C-E
20. C-E
21. N

EVALUATING CAUSE-AND-EFFECT REASONING

22. Immigration

Proposed Cause: Americans wanted to restrict immigration to "desirable" people.

Connection: It's quite logical that Congress would restrict immigration in response to public pressure. But this argument doesn't say the public actually pressured Congress.

Stated Effect: Congress passed a literacy test requirement for immigrants.

Other possible causes for a literacy test: International agreements on other issues; depression

Overall: Pressure from the people is a logical explanation for the literacy test and the most likely one.

23. Corporations

Proposed Cause: New, mighty corporations

Connection: It is logical that Americans would be alarmed by the power of the new corporations, especially if the corporations were richer than state governments.

Stated Effect: Americans were alarmed.

Other possible causes for Americans to be alarmed: People may have been alarmed by particular practices of the corporations, rather than by their power. Or Americans may have said they were alarmed when they were really jealous of the wealth in the corporations.

IDENTIFYING COMPARISONS	24.	C
	25.	C "Increased" compares production in two different time periods.
	26.	N
EVALUATING COMPARISON REASONING	27.	If "Gilded Age" means extremes of wealth and poverty, then this is a good comparison. If "Gilded Age" includes other characteristics, such as corruption, business mergers, and conservative policies, then the comparison should deal with those.
	28.	This is a very weak comparison which doesn't deal with some important differences between slavery and freedom, such as the brutality and lack of freedom of slavery.
IDENTIFYING GENERALIZATIONS	29.	G
	30.	G
	31.	N
	32.	N
EVALUATING GENERALIZATIONS	33.	This is probably a strong generalization because it would have been easy to check all the state records to see if the debts increased. Thus, it is likely to be a complete sample.
	34.	One example does not make a very strong generalization. Conditions may have been much safer at other plants.
IDENTIFYING UNSTATED ASSUMPTIONS	35.	A
	36.	C
IDENTIFYING TYPES OF REASONING	37.	C; It is also a generalization (B).
	38.	B
	39.	C
	40.	A
	41.	B
	42.	D

Part II Mixed Problems

43. D
44. A
45. D
46. B
47. C
48. A
49. D
50. C